ABOUT THE AUTHOR

In April 2019, at the age of 67, Peter Phillips was diagnosed with the debilitating condition of Motor Neurone Disease. Having been a social worker for over 26 years, he knew how the condition affected those living with the disease. However, having been a person of faith all his adult life, Peter saw his condition as a 'Gift from God'. So, finding himself confined to the home, he began to write poetry for the first time in his life.

The book you are now holding is the result of that 'Gift' and Peter's life experiences as expressed through his poetry.

DEDICATION

I wish to dedicate this poetry book to my loving wife Diana, who has walked with me through the 'gift' of Motor Neurone Disease. And Ben, our black Labrador, who slept by my bed every single night.

Thank you.

Peter Phillips

AT WAR
WITHIN MYSELF

AUSTIN MACAULEY PUBLISHERS™

LONDON • CAMBRIDGE • NEW YORK • SHARJAH

A CIP catalogue record for this title is available from the British Library.

ISBN 9781398428874 (Paperback)
ISBN 9781398428881 (ePub e-book)

www.austinmacauley.com

First Published 2021

Austin Macauley Publishers Ltd
1 Canada Square
Canary Wharf
London
E14 5AA

ACKNOWLEDGEMENTS

I wish to thank, most sincerely, those friends & members of my family, who, having read one or two of my poems, then encouraged me to have them published...

Thank you to:

Lynda & David
Claire & Caitlin & Shopna (my carers)
Rev Bob Payne
Ian Smith
Rev Zoe Heming
Rosemary, my sister
Rev Dr David Primrose
My (late) Mum & Dad
Adam, my son
Grace, my daughter

POEMS

Drifting...

I am floating on a sea of light,
The shore, from which I came, is just out of sight.
The sea reflects the turquoise sky
Serene, peaceful, naked, here I lie.

I close my eyes – listen to the oceanic tide
Dip my fingers over the side.
I hear the whispering breeze, above
Reminds me of – my first true love.

The rays awake from their moonlit trail
They cast a shadow over the yacht's main sail.
Orchestral music – strike up the band
Lie back – I'll soon be in the Promised Land!

Fish swim silently, unseen beneath the tides
They go unnoticed, only the current as their guides.
Intelligent dolphins pick up the flow,
Race alongside: an armanda – with me in tow.

Midday, the radiant sun, high in a clear abyss
Still, calm waters, the earth could kiss.
Five miles off – and I can see a whale's plume
A huge ocean: for every creature there should be room.

Now, with my body, soul and mind
All filled with thoughts, I can't leave behind
This sea of light. This turquoise sky,
For me, this will always be my battle-cry.

July 2020

George Floyd: 14th October 1973

("Please... I can't breathe")

We had nothing in common,
I am White, he was Black.
I was raised in England, UK,
He came from Minnesota, USA.
I am part of the of the landscape here,
He was turning his life around – after jail.
I live in a quaint English city,
He lived in a large, sprawling suburb.
I am 22 years older,
He was a guy of... 46 years.
                    NO...
... We had everything in common,
My blood is red, his blood was red.
I was raised on planet Earth,
He was raised on planet Earth.
I am part of the human race,
He was part of the human race.
I live here,
He lived there – just 12 hours away!
Age is not important,
We are all adults here...
                    NOW...
... the World is different.
Now, the World is poorer.
Now a white man...
Has murdered a black man... again!
Now, we all come together – as one,
Now we all DEMAND change.
Now we will NOT give in...
Now we will LOVE one another.
Now we acknowledge OUR common humanity.
Now we are ONE... under God.

George Floyd... 25th May 2020.

June 2020

My Holding Cross

(In Olive Wood from the Holy Land)

I hold my Cross and Christ is here,
I hold my Cross and Christ is near.
With my Cross I can hear Him speak,
With my Cross, I am not weak.

My Cross sits within my grip,
Christ will never let me slip.
My Cross is hanging by a thread,
Christ gives to me my daily Bread...

My Cross is not just for Holy days,
For Christ is near me all my days.
My Cross will not save me from disaster,
But when it comes, Christ is my Master.

My Cross is with me, at work, rest and play,
Christ will not leave me, He'll always stay.
My Cross is literally my lifeline to Jesus Christ,
So I may understand, just why, for me, He sacrificed.

May 2020

Walking... at 5 am in June

I walk, bare-footed, on Raddon Hills,
The early morning dew soaks my feet,
While the sheep-cut, olive green grass pricks my soles...
...As if treading on pin-cushions.
The sun rises in a cloudless sky,
And transforms from black to blue in an instant.
My dog bounds on ahead of me, loving its freedom.
As I tread carefully, birdsong filters my ears
And an early morning bee – drones by...
As a spider completes her web in the hawthorn.
Walking here gives me time to be...
... Be myself, be in solitude, be in love, be alive.
I untangle the thoughts in my head,
So, gradually, they are reformed into manageable ball of string.
The undiluted breeze enters my nostrils and penetrates every part of me...
...And I morph into the boy I once was, carefree, innocent, alive.
Ahead of me – a gate...
Will it open, or will I have to do a youthful vault?
The dog waits patiently but enthusiastically for a decision to be made.
Thank God, it opens, he is through before me – and off.
Walking on, past a rusting trailer, entwined in gorse.
Now, my thoughts go into overdrive,
A race horse leaping Beecher's Brook
Windswept for a century or more...
Stands the famous... lonesome... pine.
I run my hand over its gnarled bark
I smell the richness of its soul.
I look up, into its canopy,
A crow stares back at me...
... As though a taxidermist has finished her project here...
... Onto the next – a peacock, or a turtle dove!
In awe, I take in the human-made, patch-work landscape and...
... In the far distance – Sidmouth Gap, then sea in the distant beyond.
I bathe in the glory of Creation, whilst thanking God for this blessed place.

June 2020

Raddon Hills, Mid Devon (EX17 4AW)

Glass Room in My Head...

There's a glass room, in my Head.
Glass to the right of me,
Glass to the left of me ,
Glass in front of me ,
Glass behind me,
Glass above me, Glass beneath me in my head.
Bright, light, hot,
Distant forest, with gnarled trees, whispering.
I touch the glass – 6mm thick.
I am imprisoned.
Though the landscape beckons,
No door, no hatch, no way – out.
Encapsulated, claustrophobic, suffocating.
I listen for birdsong, for chatter.
I listen for running water, for the wild wind.
Nothing.
In my head.
I seem to float, aimlessly
Looking right – my dreams.

Looking left	–	my nightmares.
Looking in front	–	my fortune.
Looking behind	–	my failures.
Looking above	–	my heaven.
Looking beneath	–	my hell.

Nowhere to go now,
No bars, but still imprisoned.
There's a glass room! In my head.

March 2020

It is often a dangerous thing to do – to look inside one's own head, but take courage and see what is in there. Then talk about it with a trusted friend.

The Pandemic We All Ignored!

We never saw it coming... It crept up on us,
We couldn't see it, taste it or smell it...
We couldn't even hear it... though the cries were there!
No one really knows when... or how it happened
It oozed around the world... like an oil spill.
No one knew it was 'here' – we thought it was over there,
Some said it was only down South,
Some said it was only up North,
In the cities and in the towns – not in the countryside!
No, not in the country pub... we can't see it... are we blind to it?
We are told to LOCK DOWN... to stay at home.
Face masks became the norm... hiding our black faces and our white faces.
Now everyone is scared, but we are still not talking about it!
At first it was called 'a disease' – now we call it a 'pandemic'.
The nameless innocent who have died... shot, hanged, murdered.
Still ... we look the other way!!
"I CAN'T BREATHE... I CAN'T BREATHE MAN"... Then...
George Floyd died in just 8 minutes 46 seconds... in the gutter.
Minnesota took notice. New York took notice, Washington took notice,
London took notice, Edinburgh took notice, Sydney took notice...
... and the world – then – took notice...
A slave's blood is the same as your blood ... and my blood.
We demand the pandemic of racism be silenced for ever.
Black Lives Matter... SOCIETY MUST CHANGE NOW...
From Monte Carlo to Cox's Bazaar... we demand justice for ALL...
For our grandchildren and their children... and their...
For the planet's future generations... we ask for a rainbow of peace
CHANGE NOW...

June 2020

Idyllic? – No

Moonlight
In a dark sky
Dancing on a black sea
Shimmering
Highlighting
Unseen ripples.
Lights across the bay
Warm and cosy cottages.
Sitting by an open fire.
Muffins for tea.
Idyllic?
No...
No steady income.
Fishing boats redundant
Rent to pay
Kids to feed! Uncertain times,
Four generations now
Ending
Lost pride
Moonlight.
In a dark future.

April 2020

Divine Grace... Given to Me

Is grace in my heart?
Is grace in my soul?
Should I have to look for grace
Within me...?
... Or will it be given to me by God?
Grace was a gift from God at my birth and each second it enriches my life.
The gift of Sight, by which I can see His Creation.
The gift of Hearing, so laughter may be heard all around me.
The gift of Touch, so I may feel the warmth of my lover.
The gift of Smell, so I may embrace the morning dew.
The gift of Taste, so the fruits of the world can be mine.
God gave me, a sinner, His eternal grace...
So I may become as much like His earthly Son as it is possible to be...
... So I may walk the road to Emmaus with Him.
... So I may recognise Him, and claim Jesus as my own.
My very being is influenced by His grace.
I cannot walk alone... for I will stumble, I will be crushed.
I need His divine grace to steady me...
... To give me the words to utter,
... To give me the confidence – I lack.
... To uphold me when, through lack of judgement, I make mistakes.
And, as I feel my way through life...
I praise God for His grace, given to me through Christ,
... Given to me through the pain and humiliation of the Cross
... Given to me through the ever-redeeming Eucharistic feast.
Grace is not my right, for I am unworthy...
... But God has seen my inadequate efforts...
And, by His Holy name, has allowed me to inherit...
... His Grace.
So, as I press on, I pray in His name that I will be worthy of His Grace.
And that, ultimately, He will be beside me...
... At the hour of my death.

April 2020

"Come, Follow Me"

Jesus placed His hand in mine.
"Come, Follow Me," He said: MT4/19
He showed me a place nearby,
Called the Promised Land.
I gazed upon a peaceful, tranquil view,
With birdsong and a gentle breeze
The seashore just in sight.
It reminded me of the North Shore
Walking barefoot along the cool, white sands
Picking-up shells and stone smooth glass,
The dunes amongst grazing sheep,
We gazed in awe, at the turquoise sea
"Is this our world?" I asked
"Come, Follow Me."

Jesus placed His hand in mine.
"I am The Way," He said.   JN14/6
We walked the streets of despair, with the Holy Spirit close by.
We found a forgotten soul, no home to call her own,
We stumbled upon a hungry child, the light hid from his eyes
We saw a refugee, floating aimlessly across the wild, dark channel.
I turned to Christ. I shouted at Him, " Why should this be?"
He looked me in the eye and said:
"No one comes to the Father except through me."   JN14/6
"I am The Way and the Truth and the Life."
"Come, Follow Me."

Jesus placed His hand in mine.
"I am the Bread of Life," He said.   JN6/35
I looked into my own empty soul, no nourishment I could find.
No Food of Life had been given to me and I began to weep.
"Christ," I cried "Feed me."
He looked into my sullen eyes and wiped away my tears
"Whoever comes to me," He said, "will never go hungry."   JN6/35
I tried to do as Christ had said but, temptation got in the way...
I thought that I knew best, but no. I had failed the test.
For a second time Jesus stood by me, He didn't let me down.
"Believe in Me and you will never thirst."   JN6/35

Come, Follow Me."

Jesus placed His hand in mine.
"I am the Good Shepherd," He said.   JN10/11
I looked and saw a crowd standing nearby.
He spoke to them.
"As the Father knows me and I know the Father;
I know my sheep and my sheep know me."   JN10/15
A desperate woman, standing outside the group
Could not believe the words He spoke.
"Hey Jesus – How can I know you?"
"Love the Lord your God with heart, soul and mind.   MT22/37
Come, Follow Me."

Jesus placed His hand in mine.
"I am the Resurrection and the Life," He said.   JN11/25
So, I led him to the gutters, under the railway arches,
Dark, damp and cold, where the forgotten live.
There we saw the heroin users, black mamba and the rest.
Needles lay all around, sleeping bags and filthy jeans.
"Don't tell me this is right," I whispered in His ear,
"These kids, all living on emptiness and fear."
He drew close to them and showed nail wounds in His hands.
"The one who believes in me will live, even though they die!"   JN11/25
"Whoever lives by believing in me will never die."
"Do you believe this?"
Come, Follow Me."

January 2020

Those who believe that, to have a belief in Jesus Christ is a passport to a wonderful life (1st verse) may have to think again. However, those who acknowledge that Christ walks with them, through all of life's hardships, can be assured of a 'Wonderful Life' Discuss!! So often in this world, we feel powerless to change anything about ourselves or about the world around us. As we pray, 'Hallowed be your name', we find our hope and courage again. The world is not meant to be like this. In God's name, in the name of Jesus Christ, there is power for the change we long to see.
(From the Church of England website.)

Skin of the Earth!!

I have just realised,
I am, but a pimple on the skin of the Earth!
A tiny, tiny insignificant pimple!!
Which will disappear overnight.
Planet Earth is 4,543 billion years old,
Many millions of pimples have gone before me,
Many millions will follow!
Some pimples grow into 'spots' and irritate the skin of the world,
... But they soon disappear and are forgotten.
Others grow and grow!!
To become *abscesses*...
... With dreadful consequences for the planet we inherit!
They stir... causing pain growing daily.
Until, without warning – they burst ...
Then... out spills – evil of every sort...
Grey, gruesome, nasty, pus ... they march over the Earth...
Destroying everything in sight until,
Suddenly, a cure is found, and the abscess is obliterated...
... Gone, disappeared, never to return to harm us.
A pimple can replicate!!
Cloning itself, over and over and over again.
The entire skin of Earth suffocates... in torrid war!
Eventually, after many years, a remedy is found and Earth is restored.
Always be on your guard against pimples like me,
... As they appear... they may quickly grow...
... Into something you don't even recognise
They may grow to some gigantic size,
... And hang around in the history of our mind.
Stalin, Mussolini, Saddam Hussain, Gaddafi, Hitler.
So, I will remain a pimple on the skin of the Earth...
... Then, I'll fade away, when the time is right.

June 2020

A New Dawn

(In an English Countryside)

The Starling's murmuration is over now
Dusk hides their roosts,
The silence of the night – is here,
Light shimmers on the water.
And the new moon hangs in a jet black sky,
Whilst the night breeze shimmers the corn and rye.
From a distant sycamore
A tawny owl cries.
Unseen dormouse freezes.
Vixen smells the air-fowl a mile off.
Sleepy wren nestles in – oblivious.
Young badgers explore their moonlit playground,
Whilst their elders forage.
Buzzard beds down, one eye on the ground.
Rabbit conglomeration feasts on crops.
Squirrel bunkers down, till daybreak.
Tawny owl repeats her shriek
Dormouse shudders.
Leaves of the sycamore sway in the night wind.
Toad returns to his underwater security.
Woodpigeon, on its night bow, shifts from one foot to the other,
Pipistrelles – sightless, find prey on the wing.
Herefords rest under a solitary oak

As their ancestors did, over 200 years before.
Silent Night... Holy Night... nature slumbers
Then...
A distant cockerel... summons in an early dawn
The vixen, well fed now, can sleep the day away.
The sky drifts from black to grey.
Blackbird takes the lead to awaken the world.
Robin responds
The herefords awake and amble to the rivers edge.
Half moon fades as the sun rises without sound
The timelessness of the sky changes from grey to orange
Linnet, bullfinch, yellow hammer and wagtail sing in harmony.
Tawny owl calls it night
Wren searches out her daily needs.
Badgers disappear into their unseen set
The orange sky transforms to blue as sunlight reveals all of nature's secrets.
A new Creation.
A new Dawn.

May 2020

Morning Has Broken...

Blackbird sings his melody... in open space.
Daybreak brings the glow of sunrise.
Cool air, blue sky, in a milky cloudscape.
New, Spring shoots, shimmer... on the vine.
Thrush tip-toes... beak full for nesting...
She darts to her secret hideaway,
Where, in time, her brood will live, mouths wide open,
Relentlessly demanding food.
Robin patrols his territory,
Others may think it is theirs.
A flying battle ensues and the imposter is seen off.
Solitary crow lands, uninvited... hungry...
... Will steal if necessary, no principles!
Jenny wren darts from grub to grub,
Her tiny feathered tail – bolt upright.
Gone...as quickly as she appeared.
Magpie, bold in her black and white uniform,
Configures herself around the drainpipe,
Seeking out wholesome flies, spiders, and earwigs.
Her teenage youngster joins her to learn the trade.
Pigeon flies in like a Vulcan bomber,
Fat, overweight, 'grossly obese'.
Sits precariously, like Humpty-Dumpty, watching, waiting.

When an amorous admirer tries his luck!
High on the wing, buzzard – drifts.
Soaring on the currents, gazing earthward for a morsel.
Suddenly and without warning...
Canada geese appear, in a 'V' formation.
Necks outstretched, like flying giraffes!
Honking, as their captain leads them to safe waters.
Just as a fly can slip from view... they are gone.
Long-tailed tits cluster together like the Kennedy dynasty.
Chatter, swing, peck... then, they too... are gone.
A raucous gull, disturbs the peace,
Yellow beak with red spot, mesmerising beady eyes.
Searching out herring, miles from its seascape territory.
Soon, hunger moves him on to the nearest landfill,
Where his insatiable gullet is satisfied.
This unseen garden-world had no beginning...
... And will have no end.
At dusk, as starlings begin their murmuration,
Blackbird sings his melody again...
The end of a natural day, in the natural world.

April 2020

Off with His Head!

It's never happened to me before...
... But now, my head drags on the floor.
I think it started last October,
... Yeh, the day after I fell over.
O, what a day that turned out to be,
My legs simply refused to uphold all of me.
Strange, for as I hit the floor,
My bottom protested – and now is sore.
I managed to crawl to the washing machine
Put in my head – gosh, it did come out clean!
So, sitting here, on the floor,
Head detached, like my bum, is sore.
Eventually I order a takeaway...
... Not easy, when the head is round the other way
I mean, what do you say?
Well, eventually the meal arrived;
The bloke looked at me and asked how had I survived.
I said, "Could you give me a hand?"
"Sorry, mate, my next delivery is a baby grand!"
I stuffed my head with Chinese food,
Still thought that bloke was bloody rude!
So, here I sit, with no head,
Did I mention it fell off? No – O, you should have said.
Yeh, it fell off a week ago,
Now my whole body is on a go-slow.
What I could do with is some glue
And someone who knows just what to do.
I can sit here, on this kitchen floor,
As far as I am concerned, for ever more.
But eventually, someone will cotton-on...
... That my body and my head should be one
But, until they put me in the dustbin
I'll just have sit here, looking like Anne Boleyn!!

May 2020

I Am Walking Down the Street of Life

I am walking down the Street of Life,
Potholes ahead...
Holding Mother's hand for safety,
A dumpy body on dumpy legs,
Golden curls, the envy of all the girls.
A ride in Grandad's black Austin 8,
Colour had not been invented then!
But I don't notice. All front doors are brown.
Buses – you get in at the back,
A friendly conductor with sweets. I sit on a side seat.

I am walking down the Street of Life
Drama ahead...
Holding my girlfriend's hand – first love.
Half fashion-conscious, half not!
Hair over the collar:
Mother felt was "extremely rebellious!"
I am allowed to drive Dad's red Renault 12.
Colour emerges, green, red purple, yellow and turquoise.
But I don't notice. All front doors are brown.
Black and white TV gives way to colour. Snooker booms.
Friendly corner shop is trampled on by the supermarket.

I am walking down the Street of Life
Responsibilities ahead.
Holding my little boy's hand – for safety.
"Daddy, why is the sky blue?"
"Daddy, when will I die?"
Unanswerable questions filling my head.
Job, mortgage, my own car now. New kitchen to fix.
But I don't notice, I now have a brown front door.
Another life arrives. A gorgeous baby girl.
We give thanks for the 'Gift' and plough on.

I am walking down the Street of Life
Tragedy ahead...
Holding mother's hand as she slips away.
9/11. My world collapses with more force than Twin Towers.

Divorce date: 11th September 2001!!
Heartbreak, but no life lost here. Emotional earthquake of my life.
New home, with a cream front door.
See Dad for the last time, though I didn't know it then.
Tell my teenage daughter, "Come round anytime."

I am walking down the Street of Life
Decisions ahead...
To a lonely island off the Scottish coast,
To the Abbey for worship, prayer and company.
A second visit. A chance meeting, and parting.
Electronic communication from afar,
Gentle decisions are taken on line!
And two lives are morfed into one.
Chattels and a Spaniel emigrate north,
And a light begins to shine in the darkness.

I am walking down the Street of life
Emotional security ahead!...
A coming together in adult maturity.
Many laughs, but a ten-year gap in speaking to my girl!
New horizons in 'The Close', decisions complete.
We squeeze two into one box... number 6.
Chaos, give and take... to the tip!
Planned union, just a simple celebration
But sixty turn up to wish us well,
A new beginning – again.

I am walking down the Street of Life
Blue light...
Terminal illness ahead...
Through tranquil, mature years.
We walk on the soil of Africa, Israel, France and Scotland.
I support foodbank, prison... and the night time economy.
A walk to Paris for the climate. A walk to Scotland for me.
A tentative uniting with my lost gorgeous girl,
"I don't know what happened." She tried to explain.
Then, MND shows itself: how sad, just when things were on the up!
My swan song, no sympathy, my peace with Christ.

May 2020

Mirror of Life

0 to 10:[*]
I looked into the Mirror of my Life.
Saw a little, pretty boy staring back at me.
Blonde curly hair, fair skin, brown eyes,
Two tiny dimples, encouraging a nervous smile.
His breathing is strained – asthma.
He holds up his favourite toy a glove puppet, 'Sweep'!
Then... he fades from my sight!!

10 to 20:
I looked into the Mirror of my Life.
Saw a spotty youth staring back at me.
Dark brown hair, over the collar – a rebellious streak.
Brown eyes, looked at the floor.
Shrugged shoulders – but, I am sure I saw a spark for life!
A sadness that belies a zest for living.
He looks up at me and penetrates my gaze and is gone.

20 to 30:
I looked into the Mirror of my Life.
Saw a young man staring back at me.
He had a plank in his eye,
So, he couldn't see the bigger picture
A weight on his shoulders; 1898 Emporium coming his way.
A tiny sparkle, but with it comes responsibility
He looks at me: "I can handle this," he tells me.

30 to 40:
I looked into the Mirror of my Life.
Saw a guy, I wondered who he was!
The doors on the Emporium have closed forever, a new career unfolds.
Loving wife, a little boy, mortgage, but known dark days ahead.
House to maintain, three lives to care for now!
And another... great joy... a baby girl... now four.
He looks at me: " I can handle this," he *tries* to tell me!!

[*]   = years!

40 to 50:
I looked into the Mirror of my Life.
Saw a middle-aged man, greying hair around the temples.
Two young children, a loving wife but confused, dissatisfied.
Consultations with the Psychiatrist and then... ECG.
Social needs of those around demand empathy.
A fractured leg, pressure builds. "I want you to go!"
Glazed eyes look at me, then, on 9/11 his world crumbles – like the Twin Towers!

50 to 60:
I looked into the Mirror of my Life.
Saw a sad, isolated man, clinging to his faith.
A remote Scottish Island – fresh air, a fresh start.
Trying to build a relationship with his teenage daughter
As well as building a relationship in Exeter!
Upheaval, fifteen miles down the road. Union and a new life.
He smiled at me then walked his Black Lab' in the wood!

60 to 68:
I looked into the Mirror of my Life.
I saw myself – reversed – looking back at me.
Africa, France, Scotland revisited.
Walk 235 miles... to Paris, walk 412 miles to Iona.
A slow-down drawn in by stealth. What is happening?
"You have Motor Neurone Disease, I am very, very sorry."
I gaze at myself... view my new fortune and give
Thanks to God that He gave me this 'Gift'.

July 2020

Dear Reader...
This is a highly personal piece, composed in twilight years. There are many subliminal
suggestion, which only I understand. However, I believe it was a worthwhile project,
which any of us can undertake on our own lives. By including negative aspects of your
life, as well as the positive you my find the process, therapeutic and that weights are lifted,
by the time you reach your own conclusion!!
Good Luck.

A Teardrop...

A teardrop,
A dying body.
An uncomfortable silence.
Waiting,
But for how long?
Looking beyond
Nothing is clear,
Try to unravel the future.
Make good,
Put everything in order.
Yes:
I can see the way ahead?
Silence:
Within the arms of Jesus Christ
The Soul will live on.
No concerns
Eyes now closed
Let me go,
Say it:
Goodbye then,
Honour it through remembrance.
Savour it through laughter.
No regrets!
Peace is at the heart of Love.

May 2020

When I Am an Old Man...

When I am an Old Man, I want to be able to sing, out of tune.
I want to dance down the street holding a red balloon.
I want to wear a floppy hat and catch butterflies in a net.
I want to have a hippopotamus as my very own, cuddly pet.

When I am an Old Man, I want to grow my own tomatoes
Then throw them at my MP – *Smash* – right on the bloody nose.
I want to sit in my back garden, naked as a newt
And listen to the neighbours, saying, "Hmm, he's really rather cute."

When I am an Old Man, I want to knit myself a jumper
Then walk the length of Wales, where I would get a little plumper.
I would love to ride a London bus to Edinburgh and back
But jump off at Piccadilly, so as not to pay the full whack.

When I am an Old Man, I want to carry a walking stick
And hobble into hospital, pretending to be sick.
Once in the operating theatre, I would laugh and tell the truth
And to see the surgeon's face, I could well lose my single solitary tooth!

When I am an Old Man, I want to go out clubbing,
Maybe pick up a pretty woman, with whom I could try hugging.
I would buy her tobacco and a selection of Burton beers,
Give them to her... and watch... as she bursts into tears.

When I am an Old Man, I want to have compassion in my heart,
I want people to know me for being kind – and not just as an old fart.
I want people to love me, like me, everywhere I go,
And when I die, I want people to say:
"Who was that Chap? Hmm, blowed if I know!"

My New Ferrari...

I am so excited, like a child at play...
For, a brand new toy has been delivered to me today.
Well, I say 'a toy', it is more like a necessity of life
For without it, I would have to rely even more upon my wife!

I didn't order it,
No... or buy it on Amazon.
I didn't see it on e-Bay or import it from Ceylon.
It just came to me, as if a 'Gift from God,'
Alleluia, praise the Lord: "Do you think that I am odd?"

Yes, it has three wheels, shiny... and with tyres.
It has a silver frame, from which there come black wires.
It has two brakes, which in an emergency I can 'stop it with'!!
To say that I can go less than 95 mph is simply just a myth.

But the very best thing about my new mode of transport:
It has a convenient bag, so I can carry stuff, as a last resort.
Peas, newspaper, sardines, tea, coffee, even three Swiss tolls,
But I think I'll just settle for 200 *toilet* rolls.

April 2020

I Hate Poetry...

Not everyone is into poetry, I understand that.
O yes, I realise, for some, mention a poem, and it just goes flat,
In one ear and out of the other.
For some, there is nothing new to discover.

Other folk are more open than some,
And prepared to look and think about the outcome.
They realise it's not just rhyme which is the theme,
But emotions are stirred beyond a dream.

Once over the 'rhyming' hurdle,
It's time to contemplate the immortal.
Dig deeper into our collective minds,
To see if we are running on the same lines.

So, as we leave rhyme behind,
We are able to discern the true beauty of the word.
It may well shake us out of our complacency,
And make us think in a different way.

Now we are free to explore ourselves
It's not what the poet writes about. No,
It's more about how we interpret her words
And look beyond the horizon of our own mind.

Now, 'I' can look at 'me' anew,
Allow my imagination to run completely wild.
Just as the psalmist used to say:
"A tree planted by streams of water, yields its fruit in season."   Ps1v3

And, in that moment of revelation
Our very soul will reach a new depths,
Explore our mind and meet our own salvation
In the words of poetry, we never knew existed.

So God's speed, my faithful friend,
I knew we'd get there in the end.
Yes, it's good to dream of a quiet time,
After all, we can always come back to the rhyme.

May 2020

There Is an Elephant in the Room...

There *is* an elephant in the room, named 'Peace',
Carved from acacia wood.
He is silent
Motionless
Serene.
Been by my side for 20 years now...
He has matured,
Now, the colour of genuine coffee beans
...And when I look at him, I see...
...Strength, dependability and care.
He 'never forgets',
No regrets,
No recrimination.
In his small, carved eyes, I see...
Compassion, love, truth, warmth and empathy.
In his carved trunk, I see...
Nurture, caress, guidance...
... And in his carved legs, I see...
...Power, strength, greatness and noble birth.
If only my elephant could rule the Earth.
He would recognise the needs of the poor.
He would crush the wicked.
He would demand the rich share their wealth.
He would shape the hearts of ALL...
...And he would bring his own name into our broken world...
'Peace'.

April 2020

I Love You!

Come... sit next to me.
Let me feel your warmth.
Let me listen to your heart beating with love.
Allow me to put my arms around you
Come closer... comfort me here by the heat of the fire.
Let me look into your eyes...
Eyes in which I have so often found reassurance.
Eyes which speak to me of love and devotion.
Let me run my fingers through your hair...
Long, soft as silk. Black as jet.
I draw such warmth from your gaze...
For you gaze at me, as though looking for dependence.
A dependence I so wish to give to you.
You link your arm in mine,
You give back to me the love I truly give to you.
From my heart – I thank you.
Just for a moment, my mind is cleared of the world's ills
As we sit together in silence.
Listening to the flickering flames brings peace to my soul.
You close your eyes and the light begins to fade as dusk ends the day.
So, come on... I must take you out for your walk...
... Before it gets dark.
Go on then... fetch your lead!!

March 2020

Don't always believe the words you see. Keep an open mind.

Christ, in the House of His Parents...

In the carpenter's workshop,
Shavings scatter the floor while...
... Sheep gaze upon their Shepherd.
The Holy Family are gathered.
Joseph, hard at work, is making a door...
When... suddenly, his stepson, Jesus,
Cries out.
A nail has pierced His holy hand...
... For the first time.
Blood from the wound, drips onto His foot...
... For the first time.
Anne moves to offer practical help to the boy,
Using pincers, she withdraws the nail...
... Which, in time, will be driven through flesh again.
Joseph examines the wound,
While Mary consoles her beloved child...
... Unaware this would be her destiny,
Cousin John brings Baptismal water to bathe the wound.
"The strap of whose sandals I am not worthy to untie."
... While an Apostle supports the boy...
... In his hour of need...
Not knowing, this would be his life's work.

The Dove of Peace sits silently on Jacob's ladder...
While the tools of the Trinity
... Wait for a lifetime, to be tools of restoration for humankind
And, as they wait, they configure into a cross of salvation.
Unseen, but always in view!
Whilst the single, blood-red,
Poppy flowers but briefly...
... Sleep, peace and death are imminent!
In 1849, though Mr Dickens lambasted the work,
Millais gave us a new perspective of Christ's early years.
Now, we look intently at "Christ, in the House of His Parents"...
And we give thanks... for his insight and artistic skill.

June

This painting by John Everett Millais (1829 – 1896) has intrigued me for most of my adult life. The symbolism depicted in this English scene, has, for me, brought the early life of Christ alive and has been made real to me. If you are not familiar with the painting, it is worth studying it in depth, to get a different perspective on Jesus – the man. It is now displayed in the Tate Britain Gallery, London.

"Come Closer to Me"

"Come closer to Me...
Give me your hand Thomas.
Come, this is My body,
Do not be anxious or afraid.
Peter, pull back My robe,
See, here is the open wound,
No, there is no pain now,
Yes, do as you said you would
To believe...
Gently, pull back the skin,
No, blood will be spilt now.
John, Thomas is fainting,
Uphold him...
Thank you Peter...
Yes, that is comfortable now.
Why have I done this?
In order for those who will never touch Me,
Those who will never see Me,
That they, too,
May Believe."

June 2020

Twenty lines – all of which can said to have a double meaning.
Use the time available to pray in silence. Listen to what your God is saying to to you Then,
go out into your community, where He has placed YOU in the sure knowledge, He is with
you.

My Reflection

Yes, I am in a reflective mood today...
I look at my reflection, it reveals much about me.
Though it reveals nothing.
I can see myself – reversed.
Right eye is my left eye,
Left nostril is my right nostril.
Smile – genuinely given, and I reflect through gritted teeth.

Today, I am in a laid-back, reflective mood...
I gaze at my reflection in the lake. Clear, black water.
My image looks haunting, ghostly, not of this time!
A mayfly swoops down and takes a minuscule drink,
But it's enough to cause a ripple, so my reflection's broken.
I reflect upon a broken life – lived.

My mood is one of reflection today...
I glimpse my reflection in a shop window.
In the hustle and bustle of city life, I almost missed it!
My reflection mingles with models, displaying the latest fashions.
For a moment, I join their world of sophistication and glamour.
But, in the blink of an eye, I reflect on so many years – gone!

Reflective this, and every day...
I spy my reflection in the eye of my lover.
I am smiling, as though the world has gifted me a life.
Finally, my reflection gives me a face – which I can recognise:
A furrowed brow, long lashes, brown eyes, a well-groomed chin!
My reflection shows the man I am – and will be forever more.

July 2020

Doctor... Doctor!!

A visit by the doctor in the 1950s was commonplace...
"Now, breathe normally, my little man,
Let me listen to your chest,
Hmm, I can hear a wheeze in there,
Turn around, let me listen to your back,
Hmm, that sounds fine.
Alright, now your ears and your throat,
Open wide and say ahhhhh..."

Doctor Frewer, with stethoscope around his neck,
Runs his old, spindly fingers through my hair.
His dark eyes gaze over the top of horn-rimmed spectacles...
...Which balance precariously on a hairy nose.
His bald, pink scalp defines his age – he must be 103!
Greying moustache, tweed suit, check shirt, silk tie and matching
handkerchief,
All have the familiar aroma of the 1950s piped tobacco.
Yes, all old men smelt of piped tobacco.

"I am going to give him an injection," he tells my Mum.

"It should ease the breathing straight away."
New NHS, new, disposable needles, made of plastic – extra modern care.
"Now this won't hurt... keep still, my little chap.
All over – there, that didn't hurt, did it?"
A tiny bead of a tear surfaced, but was forced back.
"Would you like this needle to play with?"
Usual practice then! Unheard of today.

Doctor Frewer came to our house almost weekly.
So the story goes, he was present at my birth.
A small, 'failure to thrive' child. "We must keep our eye on him."
One visit, he got on the floor and played with my favourite lorry.
He was of his generation.
If only I'd have known his history then!
Two world wars, the Depression of the 1930s. Rationing...

43

"You've never had it so good," Mr Macmillan told the country.
Then, Doctor Frewer disappeared from my childhood life.
... But I am sure he was still caring for little boys – in Heaven!

July 2020

A childhood memory.

Distant Secrets...

I cried out... but no one heard my cry.
I shouted out aloud, but no one heard my shout?
I screamed, but no one heard my scream.
I fell silent... and went back into myself?
I wandered through the history of my mind alone,
And glimpsed the soldier who had haunted me since childhood.
I came to a darkened place which I knew well,
Standing there I remembered what had happened at this very spot.
I slowly entered that blackened place.
Before me stood the Evil One.
He was crying tears of blood and sweat ran from his brow.
He looked at me from years ago.
Agony upon his face, a trembling hand he held out to me,
And through the depth of 'our' despair he looked at me.
"Can you forgive me, daughter, dear?"
"Dad, I was ten years old!" I screamed. "How can I?
I am now seventy-one! All those blighted years!!"
I turned to go back to my wretched thoughts then glanced back.
"Yes, Dad I forgive you," I said to this stranger, standing there – long dead.
In my mind, I ran back to my present life.
A loving partner of fifty years, two daughters and one son,
... Seven grandchildren and a beautiful great-granddaughter.
I breathed a heavy sigh, of great relief. I smiled,
The first real smile, for many a long year.
"Cup of Tea – Love?" O what joy!!
Thank you Jesus for walking with me and hearing my cry.

June 2020

"Yes, I am afraid it does happen!!"

Are We at War? Again...

Yes, my brother has gone to the front...
I am worried sick about him,
My husband has been called up... to the foodbank
Don't know how he will cope, with his bad back!
Lifting heavy tins... and toilet rolls!
I'll just stay at home... and wait...
Well, you feel so helpless at a time like this.
Those deadly bombs keep raining down!!
They say London was hit last night...
... But St Paul's survived... thank God...
... And you can't see those tiny Coronavirus things!
If I could... I'd stamp on 'em. Kill 'em dead.
No one knows how long this will last...
... Or what will happen next.
Mr Churchill came on the wireless...
"Fight them on the beaches," he says...
Boris says, " Stay at home... save the NHS."
So what are we suppose to do? Yes, I am still scared...
And now, there is food rationing...
Some people are stockpiling
... Even toilet rolls!
But we'll be OK – I've got 50 stashed away...!!
I'll use my ration book to get bread and powered egg!
The schools have closed
My Jack is bored stiff
He goes and plays with his mates...
... On the bomb site, where the pub used to be!
But, as I say, I am worried sick.
The streets are empty,
The buses are empty.
The trains are only carrying troops
... And everyone is wearing those masks.
I'll make one for my Jack...
But he won't wear it... all he wants to do...
Is go and fight... like his Dad... at the foodbank.
Fight the 'Japs' and fight the virus.
They're building hospitals in a week...
For all the wounded...

For all those poor folk with that virus thing... 46,210 folk have died.*
God, where will it end?
I put a candle in my window last night...
... And I will go out tonight, clap for the nurses...
I watched Coventry burn – 40 miles away!
The night sky was a bright orange...
... I could even smell the smoke.
Yes, I am frightened...
Is this 1941 or 2020??
I am confused...

Apologies for the confusion – but that is surely how we all felt, in the year 2020.

* As of 3 August 2020.

Oak Tree... God's Donation

Oak tree twenty decades old and gnarled,
Standing in a field – Winter freeze,
Naked trunk, naked bough – upon its knees,
Barren branches, redundant twigs
Leaves, once reaching for the light
Now, dead, no life – out of sight.
Crow rests upon its bark,
Cold, windswept, twilight-dark.
Squirrel has abandoned her retreat
For warmer boughs beneath her feet
Now forlorn and solitary
Lost in history though legendary.

An early swallow upon the wing
Gives a hint of winter's early Spring.
Deep within the depths of the sapwood
Hormones stir, though misunderstood.
The cycle is rejuvenated
Like a river – it is reconsecrated.
Put an ear to the tree
Hear the water flow upwardly.
Defying gravity,
Gives life to the canopy...

Minuscule movement deep within,
Spring life is reignited once again.

New wood responds to the water flow
Secretly, slowly, new life will grow.
First the bough and then the branches,
Through the sinews, life advances.
Days and weeks wait, like a Trojan horse
As twigs absorb from life's eternal source.
Rays of early morning light
Dance on the branches – out of sight.
Emerald buds appear above,
Tiny jewels of life – unnoticed like Noah's dove.
Still more life is absorbed from the earth
And this old oak awakens, with extra girth!

Late Spring light, morning dew
Brings new life to every sinew.
April showers, cool refreshing rain
Seeps into its heart, its bough and wooden brain!
Something flicks in those inner twitches
Emeralds into oak leaves, turns into nature's riches.
More sunshine, more wind, more rain;
Crow returns, before the squirrel – again
She finds her once forgotten hide.
Now she can raise her babes with squirrel-pride
With outstretched arms this old oak revives
But wait, there is one last gift, deep inside.

From little acorns, huge oaks do grow:
So silently, as pure as the driven snow
Within each bouquet of leaves above
Appears a tiny crystal 'nut' of love.
With no mother to nurture on the branch
Nature's seed relies on nature's catch:
Sunbeams, raindrops, air from the sky
It slowly grows – we don't know why!
Crow will scavenge, squirrel can now feed
Upon the the acorn harvest, survival's need
Many an acorn falls to the earth,
Carried and buried by crow, to give new birth.

This cycle relies upon no human hand,
Not configured in factory or on cultivated land,
No scientific experiment, no test-tube embryo,
No glass-house or fertiliser to 'make' it grow.
Just nature's secret, of fertile soil
Nature's never-ending and relentless trial.
Rain and wind. Light and frost,
If were not for these – all would be lost
So feel the bark of this silent, yet remarkable being
Envisage, the intricate natural growth – all unseeing
Then sit beneath this mighty creation,
For, YOU for me, all of us – this is God's donation.

July 2020

God... "I am with you"

Where the ocean meets the land... I am there.
Where the land meets the sky... I am there.
Where the sky meets the stars... I am there.
I am the very universe of your Life.
A life, so precious, it is beyond your understanding.
A life... that has been loaned to you,
And in it... you will feel the wind of all Eternity.
You will hear the thunderstorm of creation all around,
You will see the sunlight of simplicity,
And touch the rocks of your own, unique destiny.
You can walk the path, that lead to joyfulness,
Run the road, that takes awareness by surprise.
You can even rest a while, in the arms of My compassion.
And when you look around...
You will see the tribulations of the globe that is spinning
And you can kneel beside the broken-hearted, in My Name.
Comfort the bereaved in their hour of need.
And share the words of comfort, in your soul,
Whilst holding the withered hand of the forgotten.
I will be the beating heart of that dying child,
I will be in the tears of a helpless mother,
And give strength to the father, digging a grave in the dry earth.
So...
Don't persecute the wicked – they know no other way,
Don't look down upon the selfish – for it's in their DNA.
Don't think that you are better than the next...
And don't worry for the future – for that is in My hands.
Simply do as I ask, which is in your heart,
And I will nurture, teach and guide you through the maze.
And should I call you home, prematurely,
Accept that Gift, as it is truly given,
For it will lead to your own – Eternal Heaven.

July 2020

My Kaleidoscope

Come, look through my kaleidoscope
See the light shine through – see the magic...
... Of a hundred microscopic mirrors
Come, see the world in a different way
Upside-down, right side up and inside-out.
See the colours, see the shapes
Making a glorious collage before your eyes.
Turn the 'scope just a touch...
... See the change
Amazing shapes made from the beauty of life!
Diamonds of blue, circles of red, triangles of yellow
Diagonal lines of green and brown...
Come, look through my kaleidoscope
Enter my world of illusion and fantasy
See the planet as I see it... distorted yet beautiful!
Simulates St Paul's dome! Or the Basilica of St Mark's!
Wren would have gazed in unseen amazement!
See the sky, in all its wonder its glory
Clouds gently floating upon a summer breeze...
... But within shapes we've never seen before!
Don't be frightened, do not be downhearted...
... For your world is still there – untouched.
But, this is *my* world, for the minutes of my choosing.

June 2020

On: 21st June 2020, 8am

Glance up... see the vista of the sky,
Differing hues of blue,
From the deep of a new-born's eyes, which gently...
... Gives way to the pastel of distant blue, of a windmill fan.
But the canvas is not clear, for clouds...
... Drift in from nowhere.
Where are they going? No one knows, and cares even less.
But look, they form unique shapes, which are ever-changing,
Never to be the same again...
Like an armada of candy-floss on Brighton pier.
As silent as 'nothing', as glorious as a soprano's voice.
Sometimes, a world map emerges, for just 20 seconds:
Africa, the Philippines, Haiti, Iona and Italy drift by,
As though on a global journey to Paradise.
As the sun rises from slumber, shadows are cast
Gently they move across the 'scape, seen only by lowing cows.
No destruction, nothing misplaced, no disturbance.
And so as our Creator paints our skies, with her unseen pallet...
Unnoticed, no remarks, forgotten in an instant.
Is it worth recognising this never-ending 'App'?
Or, shall we continue to ignore it...
... As we have done these last twenty years
And simply indulge in the drudgery of Lockdown life?

June 2020

53

Amnesia

O my God... my mind has gone into Lockdown – Help!!
A gossamer-thin veil has descended on me.
The view from the window of my mind – is blocked!
In my head – I am trapped in the grey walls of my prison cell.
I am searching for words in the smog of the spell-checker.
I can see them, lying on the floor – in disarray,
A crossword entrepreneur's nightmare,
A Scrabble enthusiast's conundrum!
I can't get the letters in any order!
The words are all there, but they make no sense.
Is this *my* gobbledygook?
It is chillingly sad!
Ashamedly morbid!
Will the fog ever lift?
Will the tide ever turn again?
Will I *ever* rise again?
Unanswerable questions as my brain – finally shuts down.
But wait... What is this?
A chink of memory, an atom of resurrection!
Who will rescue me? Who will pull me from the mire?
The Wordsmith – No. The Dictionary Man – No
The wordy *Sunday Times* – No.
Only my deep imagination can rescue me now.
Only the pain of the unknown – Only me.
So, come on, lift the vale, ease the lockdown,
Count the letters, which form the words,
Which construct the prose, which complete the whole.
Give faithful thanks to *All* who, in their own unique way...
...Appreciate the love and support in the words I bring forth!!

June 2020

I Met the Holy Spirit...

I met the Holy Spirit, in the confusion of my life.
I'd met her once before, but then, I didn't recognise my strife.
"What is troubling you, my dear?" the Spirit said to me,
I put my public smile on. "Nothing, I'm OK!"
"Seek help, my love, before it is too late."
I began to cry – for I knew 'the booze' would be my fate.

The Holy Spirit held my hand and led me through the doors,
"When did this all start, my friend?" – There was a long, long pause!
"My Dad gave me wine when I was just ten – for a lark!
At 15 I drank a bottle a day, sitting in the park.
By 23 – a bottle of whiskey was my only friend
At 25, I was pretty sure this would be the end."

Then, the Holy Spirit spoke to me again,
"You have nothing to lose, but so much to gain."
It seemed I have had a huge granite rock tied around my leg,
But, if I look down – nothing there – Set me free – I beg.
"I can help you, to help yourself," the Holy Spirit said to me,
And so she showed me the path I should take, for a happy eternity.

I cried and cried, as I confessed, just exactly what I had done!
A kindly guy gave me a tissue box – "Yeh, I have been there, it's no fun."
An Asian man in the group described what drink had done for him,
"Lost my wife, my kids, all of my family. The community did me in!"
Again, I felt the Holy Spirit was 'holding' onto me,
If I can see this demon off – I knew I would be free.

With overwhelming guidance from the Holy Spirit,
I was determined to take a different path... which no one could inhibit.
I had no friends, no mates in life and definitely no 'night upon the tiles',
I kept well away from every kind of booze; slowly came the smiles.
I even moved out from living with Mum and Dad and my little brother,
Rented a flat, far away, in another London borough.

Don't mind admitting, I felt just like a car-crash!!
What with no one there, to tell me what to do, and very little cash.
I applied for Universal Credit, though my computer skills were not good,
I waited six weeks, but the money didn't come, as I was told it would.
Thought of returning to 'the bottle' – but someone told me of the foodbank,
Given food to last me just three days, without it, I would have sank.

Talk about 'start again' – I couldn't believe myself!
The Holy Spirit visited me. "God Bless you dear, now look after yourself,
Why not come to church with me? I'll introduce you to *my* friends."
Listened to the sermon, songs and the prayers. Is *this* where I can make amends?
The people were so kind to me, even when, eventually, I told my story.
They prayed for me and – to the Holy Spirit, we gave her ALL the Glory...
... for this very human story!!

July 2020

Please note, the Holy Spirit walks in disguise amongst us. We may not recognise this Being, of which Jesus spoke, but with faith, an open mind and a loving heart, we can ALL be assured of God's love, through the Holy Spirit.

I Am a Slave… Today – 16 Years of Age

1. The Lord is my shepherd, I lack nothing.

I am from Myanmar.
I'm alone and frightened.
My Mum and Dad were forced to sell me.
I came here by bribery and lies,
I am in a foreign land… I speak no English.
Jesus, please come to me and hold me.
I ask for nothing else, but Your love.

2. He makes me lie down in green pastures,
he leads me beside quiet waters.

I have been beaten, starved and, yes, raped.
I will be on the streets again tomorrow night.
O, I need Jesus by my side…
Perhaps, together we can search for a quiet place where,
In my head, I will find a cool mountain stream.
How long… O Lord… before I am saved?

3. He refreshes my soul.
He guides me along the right paths
for his name's sake.

"I am with you," He tells me. "Never forget that."

4. Even though I walk through the darkest valley,
I will fear no evil, for you are with me:
your rod and your staff comfort me

But, I am afraid. I can't see the way ahead,
For it is dark and traitorous.
Jesus says, "Have Faith in Me.
No one will harm you again… not a drug dealer,
not a pimp, not even those who 'say' they care for you!
I promise to be with you,
Especially during your worst nightmares.
I will be your Comforter."

5. You prepare a table before me in the presence of my enemies.
You anoint my head with oil; my cup overflows.

So, Jesus prepares my way,
Even though the pimps are watching
... The drug dealers are just around the corner.
Then, without warning, at three in the morning,
The front door is kicked in.
There is shouting, which I don't understand.
Are these policemen?
The pimps are arrested and taken away.
The drug dealers melt away!
O... I am no longer a slave girl,
A prostitute. I am no longer a hostage.
O, thank you, Jesus...my happiness overflows with joy.

5. Surely your goodness and love
will follow me all the days of my life,
and I will dwell in the house of the Lord forever.

Jesus, Please show me the goodness and love in myself.
Guide me, where ever I go, for the rest of my life...
I promise to keep you in my heart – forever.

May 2020

This short piece (not really a poem) is based upon Psalm 23. This is my interpretation of the Psalm. In modern times, I believe Jesus is still the Shepherd of His sheep and that through Him, all evil can be overcome and we will lack nothing. Some may query why a 16-year-old Muslim girl puts her faith in Jesus!... but we all come to Christ via different routes. No one, but no one, is excluded due to the background of their birth.

Foodbank...

Yeh, we rent a two bed semi on the estate,
Married for seven years, yeh, my wife is my mate.
Two great kids – four and two.
Nine year old Ford Escort in dark blue?

Been in the same job for six years now,
Bills are paid, not much left over anyhow.
I don't smoke, I don't drink,
Spend me time at the kitchen sink!

Last February, the firm went into liquidation,
Got paid redundancy – but it changed my situation.
Cashed in a small insurance and sold the car,
Applied for Universal Credit, but that didn't get us very far.

We managed the Summer months OK,
Evan managed a little holiday.
But then – things got really tight,
Someone suggested we go to the foodbank, but it didn't feel right.

"No." I said. Till one day, I had no money for a loaf of bread.
We had a row; I lost the plot, went out right out of me head.
She went to the foodbank on her own,
I couldn't face it, I'd rather go to a 'shark' and get a loan.

Anyway, she come back with food for a week!
I cried... I've let us down; there ain't no future, it's all too bleak.
I couldn't eat the 'charity' food, so gave my portion to the kids.
I lost two stone – I went so thin, you could see me ribs!

Kept going to the Job Centre – no employment, so to speak,
But like a trooper, she went to the foodbank every week.
Got behind with all the bills,
Yeh... thought of topping myself, but only a coward... kills.

Then, one evening, a knock at the door,
It was her brother – yeh, me brother-in-law.
He'd seen a job, in a packing factory,
Not the same money, but it would be satisfactory!

So I went for the job – and to my delight,
Got it – they said I could start the very next night.
I have never come so close to being 'sank'.
I owe everything to Lichfield foodbank...

July 2020

(NB: This situation is fictional)...
Thanks to all you guys, who supported us...

There Is Whispering behind My Back

There is whispering behind my back,
Silent words, that I am not supposed to hear,
Muttering, which they think will upset me,
Secrets, kept from me, about me.
They have my best interests at heart – of course.
No one wishes to upset a dying man,
They think that I am fragile and will shatter if the truth is told.
Perhaps they are right, perhaps I am wrong
For yes, I can no longer down a pint in one
I can no longer climb 'Thorpe Cloud '!*
Or, brush my teeth, or walk to Iona in forty days.**
Yes, my legs are weak, my grip no longer grips!
My lungs have stopped performing on their own,
And my head is almost dragging on the floor!

But, these skills the world can see.
These are things I now do, to show that it is me.
The world has been taken in, as a cobra would eat a mouse!
But can they see inside my soul?
Can my inner thoughts ever be on display?
Should my wicked nature – ever be known?
Will my imagination ever escape?
Do those jealous thoughts ever show themselves?
Does the greed of my heart ever rise above the parapet?
Can my inner cravings ever be seen?
Will my sinful thoughts be my downfall?
Or, can I keep myself wrapped, as in a pig's blanket?
Can I bury myself into my own self-worth?
Can I continue to deceive, until the day I die?

Only God knows.
Only God can see inside my soul,
For it is He who knows my words before I speak.
Only He knows my inner thoughts.
Yes, He knows my wicked nature and holds it close.

    *   A steep hill in The Derbyshire Peak District.
    **   In 2017 I walked alone from Lichfield Cathedral to Iona Abbey (412 miles) in 40 days.

God takes my imagination and uses it for the good of others
He takes my jealousy, my greed, my cravings and my sin.
And forgives – with His compassionate heart – for me.
And – yes, He shields me from myself
And from the whispers that surround me.
He keeps my Spirit burning, deep inside of me
He carries me when those whispers are unyielding.
He knows my every move, before I make it.
And, in the end, as whispers cease, He welcomes me – a sinner.

May 2020

That Old Wooden Cross...

I have been forgotten, for years...
... Strengthening, maturing, drying.
Awaiting my destiny. Then, one day...
... Without ceremony, four burly soldiers come...
And with all their strength,
Lift me... and carry me to prison!
I see a man, unknown to me... Jesus of Nazareth...
... I hear them say.
Scorned, spat upon, a crown of thorns...
... Upon his head,
Dried blood in matted hair.
Sullen eyes, weak body – tired and worn.
They drag him to me.
They whip him again... and again.
From somewhere, he finds strength to lift me.
A dead weight...
I balance on his bare back, I dig into his spine.
A cry of searing pain...
Barefooted, He drags me up the cobbled lane
People jeer, shout, spit – while women cry.
Collapse, and I fall to the floor...
Blood-splattered!!

Soldiers haul me up and dump me on his back again,
More jeering, shouting, spitting, crying.
His agony-cry, stab the souls of all...
... Who have ears to hear.
The second fall, and I am again cast aside.
A woman runs out. She wipes blood from His face...
On again, up to Golgotha...
... Where He gently lays me down.
His naked body is lashed to me
Then, hard, rough, metal nails...
... Are 'banged' into hands and feet.
Jesus cries out again in everlasting agony.
I cry out... the world cries out...
Jesus, nailed, as of wood to wood...
Together, we are hauled up...
Amidst shouts, jeers, weeping!
A hole had been hewn out of the rock
I am dropped in...
... And the cry of Christ could be heard...
... Throughout the World.
"*Eloi, Eloi lama Sabachthani?*"
Pilate's 'get-out' notice is nailed to me...
"This is the King of the Jews."
I try to comfort Him.
I try to be strong for Him.
His gentleness sheers into my very veins.
I talk to him... He talks to me...
"Forgive them – for they know not what they do!"
The soldiers cast lots for his cloak...
... Whilst giving Him soar vinegar to drink.
A jagged spear, is twisted into his body...
... Water splashes to the earth below, offering 'New Life'.
Women cry...... His blood falls to earth.
He gives his Blessed Mother to another... his last miracle!
Dusk... a gentle wind cools the air...
I stand, upholding the "King of Kings!"
Then in the dead of night...
As Jesus and I stand together...
He lifts his voice to heaven and cries...
"It is finished," – so I stand on Calvary – alone.

SILENCE for 15 seconds. (Optional.)

Men and women come and gaze at me.
The hollow body... hanging... limp and lifeless.
A full day and night pass – un-noticed...
Until, a motley crew arrive...
... And with the gentleness of holy oils,
Release the fleshless body from 'my' wooden body.
Christ is released to the world, for evermore,
Whilst I am humbled...
... To become the symbol of His Glory.
The Cross of Christ becomes jewellery for the rich...
... And sustainable soul-food for the poor.
... And down the centuries I, that 'Old Wooden Cross',
becomes the promise of New Life.

(Let us pray together.)

March 2020

An old wooden cross and the beaten body of a 33-year-old man don't naturally go together! But, think of the passage of time that has past since these two imponderables were brought together – and here we are – still talking about it!! Discuss.

My Secret Garden...

I have a secret garden.
I often go there,
To find peace, quiet and solitude.
I arrive by bus – Number's 626!
"The Lord turn his face toward you and give you peace."
I am dropped at the end of the lane...
...And walk down, as far as the bend.
Turn right, along a sheep track...
...For a quarter of a mile – turn left.
It is not as *you* may imagine.
No little gate, no high walls to keep out prying eyes
No well kept lawns, or topiary peacocks.
No military flowers lined up in a row,
No summer house or small boy in a wheelchair!
No...
My secret garden – is wild with...
Orange tip butterfly, cinnabar moth, dragonfly...
...All as wild, as the thoughts in my head.
Some would say my garden is unkempt, rugged, forgotten in time.
Grasses, taller than me, gnarled trees 300 years old,
A dead elm, sycamore, a neglected douglas fir,
Wild blackberry, a harvest for nature's needs.
Around the edge is the thickest of hawthorn hedges,
Sparrow, blackbird, thrush and wren nest here.
Rearing young for the next generation.
And in the far corner, stands a majestic oak.
A trunk, wider than 'Elizabeth Tower'!
Branches that stretch almost to the moon!
Leaves, a million leaves and more... many more...
All the colour of the Amazonian forest... in the rain!
I head for the oak,
Grasses brush against my face, like silent whispers...
I push my back onto the oak and feel its hardened skin
I open my eyes and...
...I am dazzled by nature's natural colours.
Wild golden buttercups, dainty white daisies,
White ground elder waves in the breeze
Nettles, green with envy, promise to sting,
Docks promise to soothe.

Yellow dandelions sweep the floor
Before transforming into delicate, flying candy-floss.
Bindweed, birds-foot trefoil, honeysuckle, clover...
And... and... the perfect prize of all...
Blood red poppies, swaying, calling, responding to my thoughts:
"No more war, no more killing, no more 'Passchendale'."
From here, the silence deafens me.
From here, my heartbeat calms.
From here, my soul can breathe... as it used to do.
But, I am not alone, in this paradise of nature... O no...
Mr Toad comes to greet me.
Rabbits keep their distance,
As they munch the farmers crops,
Shoplifting on the job!
Stoat weaves himself around the trunk,
While squirrel feasts on acorns in the canopy.
Woodpecker knocks... but never comes in!!
Buzzard drifts on the current, high, high above her next meal.
Hot sun, clouds pass by, breeze follows its well trodden course.
Now, I return to the world.
So, "Where is my secret garden?"
Oh... it's in my head!!

April 2020

Sparrows at Play...

What is the use of a Sparrow, then?
What do they give women and to us men?
What is their contribution then?
They're not even funny, they are no comedian.

The Sparrow has such drab clothes,
His feet are drab, and his toes.
All day he sits there on the fence – just looking!!
No thoughts in his head... are even cooking

Mrs Sparrow, she's just as bad,
Sitting there, miserable and sad.
She ought to get out there and get a life,
Making Mr Sparrow the perfect wife.

Having thought about it quite a bit,
OK, sparrows are reasonably pretty, I must admit.
Their plumage is different shades of brown.
Yeh, they look like a drab, but happy, clown.

They hop around on the lawn
Eating the last few fragments of the corn.
On the feeder, they hang upside down,
It's then you see their shades of brown.

OK, so I was wrong,
Sparrows can sing a cheerful song,
And – as I sit here day after day,
I can appreciate the sparrows at play.

May 2020

Love Thy Neighbour...

I saw my neighbour last night...
... We chatted over the garden fence about the cricket score.
Nice to see Trevor, he's a real mate.

I saw my neighbour last night,
Fishing on Lake Malawi, he caught two small fish all night,
To feed his elderly mother and family of four.

I saw my neighbour last night,
Sitting with his family, under plastic sheeting ,
Waiting for his son to return from Aleppo.

I saw my neighbour last night.
The Mosquito plague has destroyed her crops again.
No food, water five miles off. Her grandchildren are hungry.

I saw my neighbour last night,
On Kangaroo Island. His home destroyed by the bush fire,
Everything gone, except a pair of trainers.

I saw my neighbour last night,
In the wastes of Siberia,
Ten degrees below, no waterproofs, no snowshoes.

I saw my neighbour last night.
She was given 'Monkey Dust' by a friend
Her life is slipping away... she is 19.

I saw my neighbour last night,
Neck deep in a mudslide... somewhere!
I watched, as his home drifted down river... gone forever...

I saw my neighbour last night,
On the streets of Birmingham – my home city –
She was wrapped only in a blanket.
Someone kicked her in the face, knocked a tooth out.

I *do* love my neighbour, but feel inadequate.
I *do* want to pray for my neighbour, but feel unworthy.
I *do* want to do something, but what can I do?
I *will* pray, but is that really enough?

Let us pray...

O God. I thank you for being there for me...
I bring before You now, ALL my neighbours of the world...
Wherever they may be... right now!
I don't know their names... but You do.
Pour out Your loving Grace on my neighbours.
Give me the inspiration, determination and the tools
To be Your Hands on Earth.
Then, I WILL serve You and serve my Neighbours equally.
This, I ask, in the Name of Your Son, Our Lord, Jesus Christ.

Amen.

May 2020

Recognising that everyone is our neighbour is a hard lesson to learn. We are asked by Jesus to 'Love our neighbour'. **Let's start to do it from today.**

Yemen – 2020 and Beyond...

Salwa al Odabei is lying on the stone floor.
At five years old, she should be able to run and talk,
But she can't.
All around her is civil war
Brother against brother... Man against man...
Principle against principle... AK45 against AK45!
Salwa only has sugar and water to keep her alive.
She has severe brain damage caused by the malnutrition.
Mother and Father can't get food... there is none!
They go for many days... with nothing.
Salwa is too weak to stand.
Her fragile ribs are only covered by her wafer-thin skin
Her bony legs will not uphold her lifeless body.
Now, there is another foe.
Coronavirus has come to her village... It is only a matter of time...
... Before Salwa, who is *your* child, will die.
Not 'pass-on', not 'go to sleep'... but she will DIE.
Salwa will be just another statistic...
... Two Million more will DIE...
Yes, turn the other way in horror! We all do!
Yes, choke on a Burger
Yes, throw away that rotten fruit.
Yes...
Carry on... worrying about the length of your hair!!
Yes...
Carry on.

NB: This is a true account of one little girl's life. Please HELP.

Globe...

Just above my armchair – hangs a glitter Globe!
Not depicting lands, oceans or archipelagos
... But tiny reflective mirrors, over 500 – I suppose.
On a Winter's day, it hangs benign, unemployed!
Come Spring, as the sunrise coincides with breakfast
The globe awakes from hibernation!
Tiny, dim reflections dance upon our eggshell walls.
Outside, blackbird and hedgehog vie for worms
... And as Spring gives way to Summer
A sunbeam, having travelled 93 million miles in 8 minutes,
Somehow seeks out – my globe!
With windows ajar, it sways gently on a Westerly wind...
... Then, without warning, tiny reflections come out to play.
Like their Spring sisters, they dance on eggshell walls,
... But with greater intention, brighter, younger, more energetic.
They look like microscopic fairies, seen, but not really there!
Blackbird sings outside, as blue tits chatter.
The globe swings. The fairies dash around the room...
And... I am reminded of our own globe world ...
... And the 7. 8 Billion souls upon it!
... It whirls around at 1,037 mph.
... While we whizz around our Star Sun at 67,000 mph.
I gaze in amazement at my globe, and all it gives to me.
I see all humanity, like dancing fairies...
Protected by the Hands of God, for all Eternity.

May 2020

Chameleon

I am a chameleon.
I have zygodactylous feet and a prehensile tail
I have stereoscopic vision and an extrudable tongue.
I climbs trees with stealth
And I love the hot sun...
...And the cool of the rain forests.
I change colour and melt into my territory.
I am me.
I can be whatever you want me to be!
If you want me to be happy
I'll be happy.
If you want me to be sad
I'll be sad.
If you want me to be quiet
I'll be quiet.
If you want me to be noisy
I'll be noisy.
If you want me to be serious
I'll be serious.

If you want me to be funny
I'll be funny.
I can listen to you, and not say a word... or...
... I can say one word of calm.
I have a shoulder for you to cry upon.
I 'almost' know how you are feeling,
I am there... but not there!
I am here... but not here!
I am holding on... with you
Looking this way and that way.
So, trust me,
I am a chameleon.

April 2020

Spider's Web

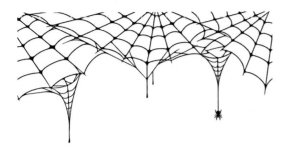

I saw a spider's web today,
And spider waiting!
Suspended from a sycamore leaf,
Swaying like a trapeze wire – precariously,
Each tiny thread holding a bead of dew.
Accurate to a millimetre,
Dainty as a cat's whisker.
As I stare in wonder, at nature's jewel,
Thoughts of my own web, come to me.
The web of my birth, a precarious miracle.
The web of my childhood, fumbling,
Denied the truth and ambition.
The web of my adolescence, to prove my identity.
The web of my manhood, inaccurate by a mile,
And...
The web of old age, observing only, a world for the young.
My web hasn't been accurate, more like a crow's nest.
So, I look at the spider's web
And give thanks for my own 'tangled' web.

April 2020

Ladybird, Ladybird

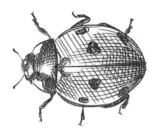

A ladybird, on the wing,
Lands silently upon me!
She folds her wings under her suit of armour,
Christ's blood spilt;
Six black spots, as raindrops fall.
She sits quietly, wondering!!
My yellow shirt convinces her
That I am a daffodil!
Her tiny legs – twitch, but she does not move.
No sound, as silent as an atom.
Then, hunger persuades action...
Determined to look for a morsel, but...
... Little chance on my daffodil shirt!
She moves characteristically over her desert:
No food, no water!
Does she have the constitution of a camel?
She is not deterred,
Even when danger seems imminent.
Arriving at my sleeve,
She seems confused by the gold cufflink.
Her own reflection dazzles her
She turns, as if on a cat-walk
And parades back – hips a-swinging!
What is going on in her insect brain?
How does she decide her next move?
For, I blink, and she is gone.
Leaving me bereft... solitary... alone,
Awaiting my next visitor... a bluebottle fly!

April 2020

Come 'Fly' with Me...

Will I... won't I?
Can I... can't I?
Here, there, up, down!
Open window... I cannot resist... in.
Like a visible, 'invisible man'!
Round and round and round... and...
Eventually, I choose the curtain as my landing runway...
Then... up and off again,
Into the kitchen, the lounge, the pantry!
Unwrapped butter, half a Swiss roll,
Fed... up, up and away,
Stairs, no problem... buzz...
A steady drone as I 'fly' to the moon,
Open doors, around bedroom one – nothing.
Around bedroom two, more satisfying clutter.
Around bedroom three, crumbs of a sandwich...
... Left on the laptop.
Another fuel stop.
The sweet-smelling bathroom draws me in...
Four times around: no food, but a discarded Aspirin!
Into bedroom three again... more sandwich crumbs.
My droning sound is music to me, but not for him!
Six feet still plied with sticky butter and Swiss roll.
Down the stairs, into the study, onto the lampshade.
Bang, wham, slam... got it!! Sorry,...
... Too slow around the circuit one more time...
Into the kitchen, the lounge, the pantry again.
More Swiss roll...
A convenient open window out into the urban world.
Next... next... next... next door.

April 2020

Bumble Bee amongst My Roses
(With thanks to: **Gordon MacRae***)*

"Oh, what a beautiful morning,
Oh, what a beautiful day.
I've got a beautiful feeling,
Everything's going my way..."

Sunlight is just tip-toeing on branches
Blackbird is feasting on worms
Hedgehog is foraging for grubs
Whilst mouse sleeps the day away.
Then... the peace of the earth is shattered!
A noise fills the space.
Like a huge electronic drone...
Something is invading this place!
Blackbird takes fright,
Hedgehog scurries for cover.
Bumble bee enters 'his' territory,
He is well overweight, his belly hangs low,
Spindle legs outstretched,
Lace helicopter wings struggle to keep him airborne.
Familiar uniform of a yellow and black waistcoat,
Two sizes too small, with pocket watch on a golden chain.
'The Poet's wife' lifts her head in delight,
Bumble bee hoovers and moves on.
'Queen of Sweden' sways in the morning breeze,
While 'Lichfield Angel' takes her holy orders.
'The Pilgrim' climbs the trellis, as bumble bee draws closer.
He steps daintily onto her golden bloom, but does not linger.
"Please Sir, may I have some me more?"
Bumble Bee ignores the request!
'Darcey Bussell' pirouettes – attention-seeking, giving him seven.
'Anne Boleyn' stands proud in full bloom.
Bumble bee, king that he is, agreed to dead-head her at noon!
Moving on, he looks 'Maid Marion' in the eye.
Oh, for whom does Bumble bee desire?
He ventures onto her pink locks,
Examines her pink petticoat and pink plimsoles.

Her fragrance mesmerises his senses.

With the gentleness of a cloud in a blue sky,
He makes love to Marion as she bathes in his advances
Bumble bee sucks at her nectar,
Whilst becoming knee-deep in her pollen.
He wants more, but there is no more of the Maid to be had...
Suddenly, she withholds her pleasures.
Bumble bee lifts his body skyward...
And, in unison, the roses bid him *Au revoir*...
"I'll be back," he calls out to his harem!!

"Oh, what a beautiful morning,
Oh, what a beautiful day.
I've got a beautiful feeling,
Everything's going my way."

May 2020

Just a bit of fun!

Daddy Longlegs

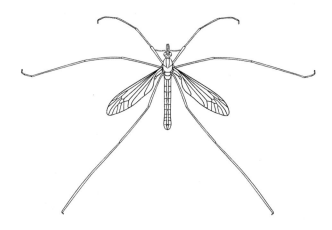

When I was just a small boy,
A long long time ago,
It was in the 1950s,
When life was very, very slow.
My time was spent in eating
My mum's home-made bread
And when I was not eating
I was in my Father's garden shed!
All day long I would search ...
... For creepy Daddy Longlegs,
Looking in every nook and cranny
Where they would lay their eggs.
Of course, grown-ups didn't like them,
But I really never knew why!!
Perhaps it was because they
Called them by their 'posh' name,
The crane fly.
My dad said they were nasty,
Calling them a pest
My big sister never understood
Why I was so obsessed.
Whenever I came across one
I shouted with delight
But my big sister simply ran away...
Completely out of sight.
So, my Daddy Longlegs,

All that long time ago
Flew all around the house,
Looking for Mum's gateau.
Its long and gangly legs,
Hanging out behind
To, my little boy eyes,
He looked so streamlined.
I remember its antenna,
Feeling in the air
Once, I caught one …
And put it in my sister's hair.
Even though I was young,
I had a golden rule:
Never, never kill one,
for I knew that it was cruel.
So, when I see a Daddy Longlegs,
At my time of life
It takes me back to the '50s,
And my introduction to wildlife.
I never have forgotten
What those creatures gave to me:
A love of all creation, on earth and sky and sea.

April 2020

Wasp in My Garden... (My Trump Card)...

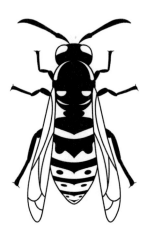

A wasp in my garden tiptoes from a blackberry to a banana skin.
I have already named her!!
Her lazy drone brings music into a peaceful, secluded space.
Dressed in her yellow and black suit,
She appears suspended in mid-air by lace wings.
Images of a helicopter, hovering over her empire!
Her waistline, so fragile, so stunning in nature.
Mesmerising eyes, always on watch for a hungry parasite.
Her wispy legs always alert for a quick landing.
She is beauty personified. The first lady of my garden.
On a hot summer's day, I throw open the windows,
And wasp has had enough of banana skins!
She hovers, three steps behind, wondering!
Eventually, mind made up, she steps politely inside.
An unwanted guest, lured by the expectation of the good life.
She tours the large white house, room by room,
Her lazy drone now annoyingly loud.
"They sting, you know – just stamp on it!" we all cry!
The first lady hovers over the fruit bowl,
Those eyes, already expecting to gorge upon on her pear!
Her waistline, fox, awaiting news, will surely slice her in two!
Those wispy legs, still dangle like dandelion storks – on stilts!
She lands upon the steps of my white house:
She has made it!!
No one knows how long she'll stay.
Most people just want this wasp to fly away,

Back to the obscurity of her garden home...
Maybe to drown in alcohol!
For from a distance she is beautiful... over there!
Come too close and she'll sting everyone in sight...
The name I gave my wasp-like 'First Lady' ?
Melania!!

May 2020

The former First Lady of the USA always reminded me of a wasp! Her elegant style always present, but it belies her terrifying 'sting'. Like a wasp, she is beautiful to look at from a distance, but close-up, she may choose to 'sting'... YOU.

God Is Waiting...

God is waiting...
He has been waiting since time began.
Long before I was born He was waiting for me.
God watched, as the fish left the sea,
He saw dinosaurs terrorise the earth,
And He witnessed their destruction...
... On the fateful day – the meteorite struck.

God is waiting...
He encouraged the ape to stand up.
He re-modelled their brain and enlarged their skull.
He placed in each one a mind and a soul!
God watched as the seas reconfigured the lands,
He saw skeletons of sea creatures form the white cliffs of Dover
... 136 million years ago ...

God is waiting...
He showed men and women how to hunt and how to gather...
... How fire can be harnessed and water can be our survival.
He provided food for all, wood and stone to build shelters.
God watched as rafts were made – to sail the seas.
He saw lives lost, trying to reach new lands...
... Some survived and colonised.

God is waiting...
A thousand millennia have come and gone.
He didn't intervene or try to control.
He simply watched and waited until
... One day, His Son came to forgive *US* – upon a tree
Many thought it was the end, but no...
It was just a New Beginning.

So, God *still* waits...
As we fly around... making profits we cannot spend...
... Poisoning the Earth – He gave to us.
Some get richer, while others get poorer
Most give of themselves in the 'Nightingales' and 'Cox's Bazaar'
Whilst a few steal that which is not theirs to have!

So, let us all give thanks to our waiting God,
In the knowledge – He waits for me and He waits for you.

June 2020

Isn't My Body Wonderful?

Isn't my body wonderful?
As the phrase goes... it is like a well-oiled machine.
It can take me where I want to go,
It tells me to rest, to restore my strength.
It only me allows to eat enough to satisfy my needs.
It keeps liquids to a minimum, whilst excess is disposed of safely,
It discards alcohol, for which I am thankful – now!
Fingernails grow slower than a glacial slide.
Toenails follow in hot pursuit – like 'Lonesome George'!
Hair sprouts from my brain...
What other useless strains are in there?
My shoulder joints hold tightly onto my arms,
My hip joints grasp my thighs – like a lucid limpet.
Whilst the knee joints hang on for dear life...
... To my calves, which never 'moo'!
Hands, fingers, feet and toes,
Are a law unto themselves. They have declared UDI years ago.
They do as they please, go where they please...
... Touch what they please! When they please.
Isn't my body wonderful?

How odd, when the machine has no oil!
Slowly, O, so slowly, limbs seize up.
Shoulder joints can hold on no longer.
Hip joints appear to have dementia and forget to grip the thighs.
The calves are well and truly encased in their pen!
Hands, fingers, feet and toes ...
... Have left the mothership and dangle lifeless...
... Like a Pelham puppet of the 1960s...

What has happened?
Even my head no longer responds to my commands!
And inside, where I cannot see, spiders have invaded me...
... Their tiny legs twitch – day and night.
But don't be down-hearted or depressed... as,
This body I call my temple still has fight left in it!
For, yes, it allows me to eat enough, to satisfy my needs.
It keeps liquid to a minimum, whilst excess is disposed of safely.

It discards alcohol, for which I am thankful – now!
My fingernails continue to grow quicker than Eurostar can reach Paris .
Toenails follow in hot pursuit – like HS2.
Hair still sprouts from my brain...
But, what the hell... other useless strains are in there?

June 2020

M.N.D. Recipient.

Inbox

I have just cleared the inbox... in my head!
God knows, it was getting so cluttered.
Messages sent four, five, even *six* years ago,
From people who have long been dead...
But who were still alive in the inbox... in my head.

They... whoever they are!...
Say de-cluttering is good for you,
So now, I can look forward to a...
De-cluttered me... an un-cluttered brain... ahhhhh!
I can't imagine what that will feel like!

Strange, but I have just banished my history from my head
Mother, father, sister, aunts, uncles, cousins, friends,
All swishing around for decades – all gone.
Past workmates, who weren't really mates at all,
Ex-wife, children, pets... all in the inbox... of my head.

Amazon, eBay, and John Lewis, all selling to me what I didn't need.
Kindly messages from kindly people, wishing me well.
War-on-Want, Greenpeace, Children in Need,
Dogs' Trust, Christian Aid and NSPCC all clambering for a donation,
They bring out my guilt. Delete from the inbox... in my head.

Press the delete button in my head: 'ping' – there, they've all gone
Oh yes, my head is free at last of every thought I have ever thought!
OK... now I can!!... but wait, what's this? BIN... 'ping'...
The haulage of my brain has been recycled. OH NO!!
The wheelie-bin in my head is bursting – once again... HELP ME!

June 2020

Thank you, Kath...

There was an old lady of Lichfield
Who bought potatoes which she tenderly peeled.
She would then purchase a number of fish,
Gut and de-scale them and pop into a dish.
A pre-heated oven the whole lot would go,
Until out of that oven an aroma would flow.
But, instead of enjoying the fruits of her labours,
She gave away fish pies to her churchy neighbours.
What a trooper, what a star, her kindness was truly revealed.
So, we give thanks for that *wonderful* old lady of Lichfield.

Eternal Care

"Take your time, my love.
We've all the time in the world.
Bless You, darling.
Call me if you need anything, darling.
Get your breath back... no rush.
Take your time, my love."

Words of kindness, genuinely given,
Words which come out of the mouth...
... As on a conveyor belt,
Words sheered into the brain...
Words with hollow intent.

For no one... just, no one... can feel my pain
Pain of the body – yes...
But pain of the heart, of the soul, of my very being.
If only I could explain, if only they knew.
Thank you for your kindness... but...

"Why don't you use the commode?
It would make life easier!
Use the urine bottle by your bed!
Have you got your calliper on today?
Have you taken your tablets?
There, there, love... bless you."

You don't get it – do you?
I don't expect you to get it...
I have been here for over 12 months now,
Maybe another 12 to go... or not... who knows.
Everyone speaks of preserving my life,
At all costs... "We don't want to lose you"...
But do I want to lose myself?
I don't know!!...

I think of eternity.
Has the time come to shed this worn-out body?
Which no longer works as it did...

Then begins the never-ending life of my soul.
The promise given to me at birth.
Each stage of my journey... different than the last!
An unimaginable peace... yes, maybe with friends,
... But more than likely – not...
Just me, in the peace of Christ's loving arms...
... As He promised to me.

"Clean boxers today, my love?
Clean shirt... let me do the buttons up for you!
Clean socks?
Which shoes today, my love?
There, you sit yourself down
Cup of tea... do you take sugar, my love?"

Kindness, generosity, sympathy
Help with tasks I can no longer do.
Genuinely given, with a pay cheque at the end of the month...
... A low wage, but not recognised as meagre...
Thank you for your kindness...
But... you just don't get it – Do you?
You just don't get it!

15th April 2020

In Memory of Rev'd Stewart Tyler who died from MND on 17th April 2020.
Aged 76 years. "Rest in Peace & Stay Safe."

Whispers...

I heard a whisper in my head,
Far away. I failed to hear just what it said.
Someone calling in the dead of night,
Looking for the morning light.
I listened for that voice again,
I listened, listened, but all in vain.
No one in the darkness of my mind,
Simply no one there, of any kind.
I closed my eyes and fell asleep,
But that whisper came again, from the deep.
I awoke and listened – a tiny voice,
Praying to God, l must make a choice.
I lay and listened to every word,
So faint, It could not be overheard.
Slowly and silently by degree,
Those whispered words, they came to me.
"Get up from slumber, do as I say,
Don't hold back, I'll show you the way."
The whisper came and then it went,
As if some sign to me it sent.
At sunrise I left my earthly bed,
And went some where in my head.
There, I prayed that I should be held,
In a place – unparalleled.
I waited and waited for a reply,
And at last the whisper did draw nigh.
It was then I realised, I was walking on Holy Ground,
With the whispers from Jesus all around.
I looked beyond the wall of faith,
And saw the sins of the world – in every place.
It was then I heard the loudest 'shout':
"Come follow Me – never doubt."
So I took the path laid out for me,
And through Jesus Christ, I was set free...

May 2020

The Secret of the Primrose...

There are primroses growing on a grassy bank,
Shaded by a three hundred year-old oak.
A rippling stream of clear mountain water
Feeds them night and day.
Their pale yellow flowers, with a deep yellow eye...
... Exotic leaves fan out like a ballerina's tutu,
Their glorious scent is a God-given gift.
Year by year, they expand their growth,
Carpeting the ground...
A covering for spiders, ladybirds and woodlouse.
Bees seek out their nectar and pollinate the earth.
Primroses often transform our communities,
Reaching out where other floral weeds fear to tread.
In their unique style, they gather in – the forgotten
The deprived, the blind and the lame...
... Allowing joy, laughter and singing to thrive once again.
Some primroses teach our young, in their hour of need.
To relax, they walk black Labs around the pond.
Other primroses show compassion in a hostile world,
And recognise that sin exists in every human frame.
Primrose seeds fly upon the wind to far-flung lands
Where they give of themselves to...

... Our Antipodean brothers and sisters.
Primroses are loyal to those to whom they answer,
Confidential in every aspect of their lives.
They care for their own, until life has ended...
... And 'return' to console and put their arms...
... Around the broken and bereaved.
Primroses acknowledge God lives in the world,
And that He created everything within it.
And to this end they live each day to His glory,
Hugging the world for those who cannot hug it for themselves.

June 2020

Dedicated to Revd Dr David Primrose & Dr Alison Primrose, for their care, compassion & devotion to the community. Thank you both...

Waste Ground...

Each morning, I pass a patch of 'waste ground':
A rusty bike, a Sainsbury's trolley, bricks, rubble and a toilet seat.
Tall grasses sway in the morning breeze,
An armada of nettles wait for their next victim,
Whilst the dock is alert to sooth the sting.
No one gives a second glance here.
"There's now't there, but rubbish," they say –
And they're right!
I stopped today – to look at nothing!
And saw Byron's delight:
"A host of golden dandelions!"
Carpeted the ground, like forgotten sovereigns...
Each flower that opens, has 10,000 petals
... Of pure joy...
Each smiling, giggling from their forgotten grave.
And daisies... open at sunrise – close at sunset...
Delicate... so delicate... white petals, tinged with pink tips...
... Surround the bright glow of a sunshine centre.
Green leaves are ground-bound...
Showing off the energy of Winter hibernation.
Tradition has it, lovers make daisy-chains...
But not here... not on this waste, forgotten ground.
Spiders, ants, beetles, forage here.
Bees, wasps, hover flies, butterflies and the night-time moth...
... Sweep in, searching for nectar...
... And buttercup gives up her delights
With her usual grace, to reveal a golden communion cup.
"There's now't there, but rubbish," they say,
... But they are wrong... In this forgotten space
The unseen glory of nature's best is ignored here...
On a patch of waste ground!

April 2020

NB: Colours: sun, sky grass, earth.

95

My Life...

Walking the rocky road of Life,
I stumble
Not through drink, just weary.
Looking back,
I can see life's potholes,
Grazed knees, mistakes, catastrophic errors.
I can hear past voices
Telling me to take a different path.
Advice given,
But rejected.
I want to plough my own furrow.
Alone.
Human nature gets in the way,
Temptation
Body to body.
Singular pleasure, but it soon disappears.
Re-start, there are plans to plan!
Aspirations are possible.
Work towards a single goal... but,
I fall again
This time, I can't get up without help.
I search for a hand to grasp, but it's not there.
Looking around, I am alone.
My eyes close – without me telling them to.
The darkness is as black as a crow's plumage.
Then... after timeless time and...
... Without fanfare, light breaks through.
Sunbeam, eight minutes to travel to me
And lasts a lifetime.
A cool breeze signifies a future that I can breathe in.
And there *is* a hand – held out for me.
I struggle to my knees and look up:
A gentle smile, a strong will.
Plans start to come together,
Though it is nothing to do with me.
I am helped to my feet, to stand tall.
The future looks... possible.

(Don't ask me... you will have to work it out for yourself!)

On the Shore Line...

I wish I was a crab walking sideways on the beach,
Sun and sea and sand always within my reach,
Rocks to climb, pools to explore...
When you're a crab, who could ask for more?

I wish I was starfish just sitting on the sand.
No, I don't sting, so pick me up and hold me in your hand.
I will not bite... but I will smile as you return me to the pool,
And once in the water, I will amaze you by looking like a jewel.

I wish I was a limpet, super-glued to a rock... no, haven't died!
Still and silent, I am quite content to wait for the incoming tide.
There is plenty to eat, if it happens to come my way
And once the sea comes in, I'll be on my way!

I wish I was a jellyfish, looking innocent in the sea,
Waiting for an unsuspecting child's foot to tread on top of me.
That is when I get out my tentacles, as I am very annoyed
And I usually resort to stinging – yes, its a pastime I've enjoyed!

So, the next time you walk along the shore,
See what you can find in every rock pool you explore.
Open up your eyes to every creature, living within the sea
And marvel at Creation and ask, "How can this be?"

April 2020

The Egg & Spoon Race... of Life!

"Are you ready, in this lovely sunshine?"
"Thomas, please get back in line."

       ... Father of two, qualified as a civil engineer.

"Kenny, no, you can't wear your sister's hat."
"Jennifer dear, don't do that!"

       ... Mother of four, helps out as a 'Foodbank' as a volunteer .

After giving her epistle,
Miss Pailling blows her whistle.

       ... Now Mrs Harrison, retired, living quietly with dementia.

And we are off – like a shot.
Class four ran as out of the pen at Ascot,
Each holding a silver spoon.
At sports day, on a Friday afternoon.
Some have practised, but most are unrehearsed
And Sarah drops her egg first!

       ... Qualified as a doctor, now works in Jamaica.

She looks aghast, but is not deterred...
As Stewart pushes through the thickening herd.

       ... Is serving life for murder in HMP Rampton.

Tony drops his egg, and thinks about the chick inside and due to his
compassion – he starts to cry.

       ... A parish priest living in the suburbs of Southampton.

Brian is steady... his dad looks on. Will he give him another black eye?

       ... Hits his wife and three girls, works in a factory, making toys.

Maureen looks at her mum – and drops.

    ... Mum died, flew to Sydney with partner and her three boys.

Reg challenges Stewart, but gets a murderous look... and stops.

    ... Divorced – now a London taxi driver.

Sonia puts her thumb on the egg, but it still falls to the ground!

    ... Gained a degree in music and now teaches – she is a survivor.

Caroline strides out, egg perfectly balanced, and she makes no sound.
She dashes through the slowing pack,

    ... Died of a brain tumour, leaving her partner and seven-year-old daughter.

Stewart still leads, but she is on his back.
Vivienne falls; spoon and egg fly into the parent crowd.

    ... Married a farmer, now lives in Lower Slaughter!

Sally falls over Vivienne, and screams out loud.

    ... Has four children, settled in Vancouver!

Kenny walks slowly, deliberately egg on spoon.

    ... At 16, realised he is gay. Works at Premier Inn, in Andover.

No one can catch Stewart now, the race will be over soon.
He stops at the finishing line.
Mum & Dad gives him the thumbs-up sign,
Stewart shouts, raises his arms in delight...
And holds his spoon and relishes the spotlight,
And the egg remains firmly 'stuck 'in place!!

April 2020

A Two in One experiment!! *Now, what is going on here? The Colour Green represents new birth, new life, a life to be lived. The colour Red represents adulthood and how we live out our lives – unplanned. The whole poem can be read together OR Green can be read separately from Red. It is a difficult, thought-provoking read, which demands a response over a cup of coffee... I think. Or something stronger! Once read, I know, you're confused – I was writing it! But perhaps it makes us realise, just how important – or not – our childhood experiences are, and how they influence the rest of our lives.*

Over the Isle of Mull... by Bus

I caught a bus yesterday,
Like a four year-old, I made for the front seat, top deck.
Tommy took my fare and...
... Wished me a pleasant ride!
A turn of the key and the engine chugged!
I swayed, as we left the station...
Slow speed changes into steady speed,
A chug quickly changes into a bus 'purr'.

Ensconced in my own 'Tardis',
The blue of the sky mingles with the white, playful clouds.
Gnarled roadside trees stand firm, as for 100 years or more.
Verge-side flowers scattered in the rainbow colours of nature.
Undergrowth of deep 'Robin-hood' green.
A cottage: who lives there?
Grandma in a pinny, perhaps.
Post Office on the left, a lifeline for grandma!
Up a slight incline, over the brow... and...
a loch... stretching to the horizon...

A cormorant fishing for survival, a skylark, unshaken by time.
Crow and seagull vie for a morsel.
Dr Johnson came this way, centuries ago.
More ancient trees line the ancient track
They saw the birth of the combustion engine...
1908 Ford Model T... travelled this route...
... And suddenly the vista changes... rounded hills
Distant snow-capped mountains, light of purple,
Streams of pure water
Flow through burnt-orange bracken. Harris Tweed landscape.

Tommy puts his foot down – a touch...
Overhanging branches crash – above my head.
The noise is frightening, but I am safe in my own steel can.
Highland sheep – graze. Not giving us a glance.
Lambs gambol, not knowing the odds!
Up, up, Tommy pushes us into second gear.
The bus roars...
At the summit of the incline, another vista to take in.
The wide open sea, meeting the blue of the sky
A seaweed coast line, derelict fishing boats...
... A heron scouring the shore.

More crofts, updated with TV aerials and mobile phone masts.
A long straight road ahead.
Tommy cruises into fifth gear. Speeds up to 35 mph.
Way ahead... a brown spot! What?
Tommy reduces his speed to 20 mph!! What is this,
Defiantly blocking our way?
200 yards in front of us, the easily recognisable,
The friend of all tourists, a Highland Cow!
Down to 5 mph and Tommy sounds the horn.
10 seconds later Ms Cow gives us a cursory glance.
With her own horns, the creature of our heart's desire,
Has no intention of moving.
The bus stops and Tommy leans on his own horn.
We too can be defiant
Nothing... no response.
Eventually, Tommy leaves the protection of his cab
And...
Talks to the cow, as a father would to his teenage daughter.
Without drama, our Highland mascot ambles to the verge.
A cheer goes up from my fellow passengers.
A turn of the key and the engine chugs!
I sway, as we continue our pilgrimage.

I return my gaze to the ever-changing vista...
Sea, dancing waves, swaying seaweed,
Another heron stalking for survival.
Pied wagtail, lapwing, kestrel, herring gull,
Ducks, misled by sea-water.
A stealthy otter fishes in a ring of bright water.

Another isolated croft, sheep grazing at the door
I fancy myself living there, but there is no supermarket nearby!
A journey of 35 miles. Almost two hours...
London to Majorca, but no Mediterranean sun here.
"You have reached your destination."
"Thank you Tommy... You are the star of the show!!"
"Hum, been doin' it 20 years... man and boy...
I should know me way!"

I have undertaken this trip twelve times – there and back.

April 2020

A Life... Unknown to the World

A miracle has happened, just moments ago...
Silence, then an intake of breath and a scream for life.
Tiny fingers stretch out to feel the earth,
Ten tiny toes, ready for a lifetime of transportation.
Eyes tight closed. Not yet ready for the world's colour.
The first touch is mother's skin:
Soft, warm, recognisable.
The breath of life now filling tiny, unseen lungs.
Intricate ears, hearing but not knowing.
...And lips which demand mother's milk.
Naked body, exposed to the cold air,
Wrapped in a makeshift blanket.
The tarpaulin blows in the monsoon wind,
More rain is threatened – later.
At last, linked to mother's breast and the warm milk flows.
Blood begins to surge around the tiny body...
6lbs 2oz, at a guess.
Curled hair, as fine as silk.
And, without warning, eyes are open...
Blue as a tropical sky...
... Soon to turn brown as a coffee bean.
The wind hurls around – rain...
To the newborn this is life as it is going to be.
To the refugee parents, this is life as it should not be!
No home, no food, no money, no future.

Bombed out of their home, now fleeing the bullets.
Asleep under the tarpaulin: the wind howls and becomes a demon
Here comes the rain... a noise like a thousand horses' hooves.
Temperature drops to minus 4 degrees.
The unnamed life is slipping fast... cold, wet, this is no place to be.
By morn it is all over.
The storm... the night... the life...
Unexplained, known only to God...
(Silence please, as we give thanks for a life... unknown to the world.)

May 2020

Can you recall the moment, when you realised this birth was not taking place in an NHS Hospital in the UK? Can you recall your 'inner' reaction, when you discovered this baby was born under a tarpaulin? And did your heart cry out, when the baby died? I know mine did.

I Am in 'Lockdown' – Virtually!

I am in Lockdown
I have been told so by father Boris,
So, I can't go out!
Stay at Home, Save Lives, Save the NHS. I can't go out!
No shopping, no meeting mates in the pub,
No running in the park... now here's the rub!
Social distancing – the length of a broomstick handle
I can't go out!
Staying in, reading newspapers, slopping around in sandals,
Eating Pringles all day long,
Listening to the birds in song
Looking at the grass grow longer!
And ... I STILL CAN'T GO OUT ...
... Though in my imagination I CAN!!
For my mind can take a virtual tour of the world – right now...
Catch a virtual train to the virtual airport,
Walk through virtual customs without a virtual care...
Straight onto the virtual 747 – I can go anywhere,
On twenty tons of virtual fuel!
I can't go out...
Though within minutes, I am sitting next to a virtual pool
... in Barbados... virtually!
... Sipping on a virtual straw, with virtual sand in my virtual toes,
In the arms of a virtual woman who has a virtual Roman nose.
I can't go out...
... But I can go trekking in the virtual Himalayas...
Back pack, sturdy boots, and a virtual guy called Andreas.
My virtual friend, the Sherpa, knows the virtual way.
I can't go out.
... But I can visit Rome, Paris or Madrid.
I can sip a virtual ice-cold beer on the virtual Champs-Elysées...
... And take in the virtual view from the virtual Eiffel Tower!
Stand, virtually alone, in St Peter's Square or Plaza Mayor!
But I STILL can't go out...
I can virtually go to the Arctic and search for virtual polar bears
See if I can see a virtual penguin or two!
Walk over virtual ice and snow and...

... Slip into a virtual ravine... h e l p ... h e l p ...
I am virtually slipping down a virtual deep, deep hole ... h e l p...
Hmmmm – I think I'll stay in Lockdown!!

May 2020

My Cross...

The Cross, on which Christ died for me, stands tall, solid and firm.
It is so close to me, night and day... I often take it 'out' of Church...
...Along the busy streets, into shops, pubs and takeaways.
I carry it everywhere I go...

I ponder upon its history and what humanity was given when He died.
I take it into the darkest places where
Christ is never seen:
A prison cell, addiction meeting...
'Foodbank' and a probation hostel.
I take it on the bus or a crowded train.
I sit there quietly with my Cross and see who sits beside me.
Then, without a word, I pray for them today.
I walk down a city street, passing a hundred
Strangers – every minute.
I can't pray fast enough, but I still have my Cross!
I stand on the congested Underground, my Cross still by my side
... I stand, holding tightly to the safety rail, looking right and left.

Beside me now... the whole of Christ's created children...
... Living their lives without knowing Him.
Not knowing... what He did for them...
Not knowing... what He is doing for them – Now!!
I trundle home... the Cross still with me.
A hot shower and a change of clothes.
I look down at my right leg.
There it is... My Cross of Christ... TATTOO!!

May 2020

Pandemic is Here... Don't Panic!!

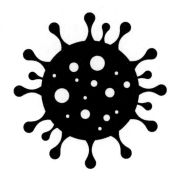

A virus has escaped from a wet market,
So what!!
It's in China... where is China, anyway?
Its claimed lives... yeh, but they were Chinese!!
We took no notice.
Somehow, the virus flew over the French Alps and began skiing!
Then it arrived in Calais. No one cared... So what?!

Can a virus swim?
No, but it can slip, unnoticed, onto Eurostar!
It arrived at St Pancras, with no ticket!!
But no one saw it.
Suddenly, English lives were lost... and we sat up!
It is passed on by a cough or a sneeze.
It sits on a bus, lies on a door-knob, hides on a park bench.
It goes into the supermarket...and out on a trolley...
Home in the car, and sits in the kitchen
Wear a mask – that'll stop the little bugger!
The PM goes on TV. " Please stay apart."
More lives are lost.
Loved ones denied a 'goodbye'!
Funnyman PM... now looks us in the eye.
"STAY AT HOME" – or we will put you in jail!
Nightingale Hospitals are built in a week...
London, Brum, Cardiff, Edinburgh.
Gowns for all medics, but in desperately short supply.
Social distancing, not a request – a DEMAND!
"STAY AT HOME" talk via the laptop.
Don't fly, don't shop, don't go to the pub,

Don't visit Granny, don't go to school,
Don't go to work...
What are we supposed to do then?
"Work from home – save lives."
2 304 have now died, but
Still the virus invades.
Only exercise or walk the dog. No sunbathing, that is an ORDER!!
Essential carers still do their essential tasks.
Church buildings close, but church carries on.
Virtual church comes to me... albeit through wonky wires.
10,000 plus... We mourn their passing, only TEN at a funeral,
Heartache, tears, we can't say our goodbyes.
But virus pushes on... to the Isle of Skye and beyond.
Care homes become God's waiting room...
Mr PM has a cough and a baby at the same time.
Self isolation, then into St Thomas's, intensive care.
Underlings take over – Gove shudders, as we all wait.
16,748!!
Multiplex closed, McDonald's closed!
Social distancing – still a DEMAND... two metres apart
Trains are redundant, planes have nowhere to go!!
Home-made face masks won't do!
The PM leaves St Thomas's behind,
"I wish to thank everyone who saved my life."
Gove breathes a sigh of relief!
22,514...
In the Spring sunshine, you MUST stay inside.
... And we all go to church – virtually.
US President suggests we drink bleach!
Doctors tell us not to... or we'll die!!
Laura Kuenssberg asks difficult questions...
"Well Laura, thank you for your question...
Er... um... over to you, Chris!!"
Food-banks are overwhelmed...
Social Security is deluged
A million claim for Universal Credit...
To buy food that isn't on the shelves
The corner shop back in our hearts.
The Chancellor climbs the wall!!
28,021...
"We are going in the right direction!!"

Yeh... and pigs will fly!!
Potatoes rot in the ground.
No one to pick the tomatoes!
The High Street is dying, as Amazon thrives!
A landmark is reached with such pain for the nation.
Her Majesty urges us to unite.
Now over 30,000 have wept to their death...
The number is rising each day
And now we wake up:
This is SERIOUS for all.
So we come to this day, just like any other,
The pandemic we're told is still with us.
Lockdown is tentatively lifted,
But we are all dubious now...
This story is on going... I'll finish it later...
Or... maybe I won't... You'll have to do that for me...!!

May 2020

The Day Prince Philip Winked at Me...

24th March 2016!!

The other day Prince Philip winked at me,
I had invited him to my place, for tea...
Before he arrived he had another arrangement,
Opening a library and unveiling a pavement!
The crowd was huge to see the Prince!
I am only small, so big crowds always make me wince.
In order to get a really good view...
I ran ahead of the crowd, dressed in Royal blue.
It was then I realised my sight would be blocked,
So, I looked around, to save being mocked.
Yes, just ahead of me,
Stood a noble sycamore tree.
Fortunately for me,
There were low branches on that tree.
I climbed and climbed almost to the top,
Once I'd started... I could not stop
But what a vantage point it turned out to be,
For when the Prince came, he looked up at me.
He gave to me a little smile,
Strange that, as it wasn't his usual style.
"Come on down from your vantage point,
But do be careful, don't break your knee joint."
So I climbed down tentatively
And stood before him, and he before me.
"Go and put the kettle on and I'd like a slice of cake."
"Yes, Sir, cucumber sandwich?" " No that'll give me belly-ache!"
I ran home and did as I was commanded,
And Prince Philip came, and with me he was quite candid.
He told me jokes I'd previously heard,
And I explained why I was called 'Peter the third'.
When it got to half past four,

The Prince asked for cake, but there was no more,
So he got up and summoned his valet – then winked at me.
"Well, I suggest you go back to your tree...
... And I'll continue in my role as Royalty.
Bye then, Mr... Mr... er... What's this chap's name?"
"Goodbye, Sir."

May 2020

24 Hours... in My Life Now

I am connected to a tube, which penetrates the nose...
...And another through which fresh air always flows.
I have a contraption connected to my leg!
...Which ensures I don't slip on any scrambled egg!
Cream is applied to my back, morning, noon and night.
No Strawberries, though,
What, strawberries on my back? I *would* look a sight!
I use an old person's cutlery to cut up my meat,
Nine times out ten, I spill gravy on my feet.
Also, I am prone to choking every now and then,
When it happens, I refrain from eating... apart from Pringles!!
Preparing for bed is really quite a nightmare,
I have support, who tells me what I should wear.
I shuffle to the loo and back...
...Then, at 9 o'clock, it's time to hit the sack.
I shuffle to the single bed and sit upon the side.
My legs are then lifted – God, it feels like suicide.
The ventilator mask is glued to my face...
...Air penetrates my lungs and I am in cyberspace.
Again I have to shuffle, this time up the bed,
Pillows must be just right, or I'd rather sleep in the shed!
A loving kiss and a reassuring hand,
I say that I am sorry, for everything I demand.
The lights go out, I am all alone in the dark...
...Sometimes, just to make me jump, Ben will give a bark.
I go to sleep quite quickly, but I am soon wide awake:
It's half past one, five hours to go till bloody daybreak.
My back complains, and my feet.
I have a nightmare that the Devil I will meet.
He stares at me and I stare back:
Why does he always wear that dirty old mac?
Come the morning and I am up,
First hot drink of the day, builders' tea in my doggie cup!
Another fifteen hours connected to this machine,
But without it, eventually, I know, I would no longer be seen!!

25th May 2020 (Amy's 10th birthday)

The Planet with No Name

In prehistoric times,
Our Neanderthal cousins sit, gazing
At an un-named orb
Which lights the night sky.
In the hours of daylight
It is not given a second glance...
... It being was so much part of the hunter-gatherer life.
By its never-fading glow,
Families relax and talk,
Language spoken for over a million years.
Beneath, its beauty is never questioned.
The ebb and flow of the tides still not understood.
... Because it was and would be for evermore,
They point to it, in the night sky,
Realise it's rapid terrestrial transit.
They put it down to nature, that seraphical spinning being.
As silent as snow, as untouchable as a snake's venom.
That near-distant planet would be their god.
Unending, yet it never had begun.
A deep, perpetual presence,
Guarding, guiding, thrilling, willing...
And over the long slow generational overflow
One or two may have argued as to who put it there.
Theoretical stories would emerge...
And told to children's children,
So legend it soon became.

Millennia past to the ancient Greeks.
Who saw a god in this night-sky globe –
And named her Artemis
...A goddess of protection.
Astronomer Thales observed the Solar Eclipses, but realised it just to be –
A lump of rock,
Which acted as a reflection of the sun's rays.
A revelation indeed.
One, since, we have taken for granted.
But some have seen it as a romantic being,
With influence far beyond its 'rock' status.
They claimed it for the Earth as an astronomical body,
Which acts as our permanent satellite.
And for over three millennia
Have used it as our agricultural own.
Harvest moon, hunger moon, storm moon, full moon.
Ancient man worked it out.
Having been so ensconced for over four billion years,
Earth and Moon were now inseparable;
Synchronised rotation, one with the other,
Each celestial city vies to be the brighter
And it is now gravitational influence realise ocean tides,
Even a lengthening of Earth's days.

In the 18th century, from English society
Came Men of Learning
In a smoke-filled upper room
Darwin, Wedgwood, Boulton, Watt and Day met...
So 'The Lunar Society' was born, with
Theories exchanged, ideas put forward...
Ideas which became the DNA of society and the world.
Did Armstrong ever imagine?
Could Aldrin ever have known?
Was Collins a daydreamer?
For it would be these three
By which the mystery would be blown apart.
Man's thirst for adventure,
Galactical exploration began with Gemini,
And was superseded by Apollo.
The promise of a dead, but great, President,
Kickstarted the race with another noble nation.

Global experiments perfected their method,
Three lives were sacrificed –
But there was too much at stake, no going back now.
Eventually, Apollo 11 left earth,
With an Eagle aboard.
We were in trepidation, holding our breath.
The moon knew nothing of its invasion – and cared even less.
Eagle detached its self from mother ship,
As Armstrong himself took control.
Alone no longer, worldwide millions watched
As he steered us into a new age of exploration
Onto the virgin Lunar surface...
... And with tentative steps, the first human descended
With unforgettable words...

"It is one small step for man but
One giant leap for mankind."

So, is that the final deadly game? Surely not.
For there is to be a future...
There will have had to have been a past.
The past can be observed...
The future we can only guess.
Sadly, our reputation lets us down,
For, wherever we go, we leave a trail of disruption in our wake.
Don't go... beauty and uniqueness should remain...
Go and we leave behind us, plastic, metal
Toxic chemicals, gut-wrenching fishing wire,
Tin trays, electric cable and clothing by the skipload.

So, let us not go there.
Let us leave our virgin moon to be just that.
Let us listen to our inner voice this time.
Let us follow our natural instincts.
The the next four billion years can be like the first
And we too can, as in prehistoric times,
Sit, gazing.

50th Commemoration of the moon landing, 20th July 2019.

Cirrus, Stratus, Cumulus and Altostratus

Sitting here, marooned...
I gaze due South, upon a wide open sky
Like my mood, the vista is ever-changing.
Cirrus, stratus, cumulus and altostratus clouds
Dash across 'my' sky...
Like a convoy of cotton wool blobs!
Unrecognisable to most mortals... but to me!!

Suddenly, an enormous white rabbit winks at me!
A slender woman floats on air.
An old man with a twisted nose passes by.
Then a white elephant, followed by a pure white chicken...
O, there's a monkey holding a banana...
and a mouse with a long white tail.

Silk-like clouds drift from right to left
... From South to North, following the unseen jet-stream.
High above...
A grey antelope dances past... and another old man.
Somehow, death is in the air...
As a young woman lying in her coffin,
Eyes closed, drifts into view...
... A funeral-like procession.
Then, her child...
Billowing tears of sadness, in a blue sky!

Grey, almost black fingers, spindle into sight...
They threaten doom and gloom.
But no, they pass and within a minute or two...
Bright, elf-like creatures run in sheer delight.
Another white rabbit, and... what is that?
A hippopotamus, with pink eyes, I do believe!
It smiles at me and brings joy to my heart.

So the clouds keep on rolling...
A never-ending picture of unmentionable beings...
Are they real? Or are they in my imagination?
To me they are as real as my shirt sleeve,

... Floating by on a sea of blue.
No beginning – no end...
But what do I know now?
How can I distinguish?
In my state of mind!
Sitting here, marooned...

March 2020.

Imagination is a wonderful 'Gift from God'. I believe.

Black Is All Around...

Black crow lands on the roof and stares glares.
Stands on one spindle leg, then the other.
Black cat sits under the blackberry bush... waiting,
With only death on its mind.
Blackbird pulls a worm from the lawn,
Oblivious that life is about to be snatched away.
Black clouds gather in a sullen sky.
A distant howl can be heard from black dog.
Black rat slips back into the drain, back to its dark, black world.
Black widow spider spins her web in order to enslave and kill.
Black fly is entangled and the widow strikes.
Black ants, 50,000 in number, work as one to build a fortress.
Black beetle wanders in, is entrapped, life is sucked out.
The oil-black sea, rages through a bleak, black night
Great black-backed gull has a beady eye on anything that moves.
Suddenly, a defenceless kit is spotted.
Survival for one, death to another.
No moon, no stars, just black clouds, the blackness of the blind.
Walk on Blackpool beach tonight, no donkey in sight
Just ghostly shapes of the black breakers defending the shore
Only the silhouette of lovers looking for love.
Black Sabbath, "Never say Die".
Come inland, Black Country folk are proud of their heritage.
Ironworks, foundries, forges and coal... but black no longer,
Now shopping malls, car parks and pizza places for the unemployed.
Six black ravens strut their stuff on the Tower wall.
Fly, superstition tells us, and the crown will fall
Taking with it, all we know, into a black hole.
So, what of the future?
Black for the homeless, the refugees and the migrants.
Black for the poor, the disabled and those forced into care!
All we can do is gorge on black pudding!!

December 2019

The Nurse

Nurse, I need to go to the toilet.
Nurse, I need you to pull up me pants.
Nurse, I need you to feed me.
Nurse, I am slipping fast.

Nurse, you are so good to me,
Holding my catheter bag.
You smile at me as though we were in love,
You hold me as a mother caresses her baby.

You never complain about the hours you work
Or the shifts you have to change –
You talk to my wife in motherly way...
... Telling her I'll be okay
When you know I am on my way out.

You give respect to matron and the consultant too.
You know exactly what they plan to do...
... And you tell me,
To ease my anxiety.

I wouldn't have managed this cancer, if it hadn't been for you.
I would have given-up, long ago...
Leaving you to re-make the bed...
... And move onto the next.

But what have I ever done in return?
Have I ever shown you gratitude?
No.
All I have done, is put you down,
Judged and criticised.
All I have done is sent you down life's gutters.
Shown you the dark side,
The black of blackest side,
The death side of life.

All I've done is to show you the wheelers and the dealers and the black mamba.
I've shown you the uppers and the downers,
I've shown you the dodgy places around...
... The derelict buildings, the railway sidings, pubs, clubs and party places.

I've tempted you.
I've said, "You can owe me, pay me back fourfold next week!"
I've even lied to you, by telling you – it was safe!
I've dragged you down, deeper than the deepest depth...
... Lower than the lowest place. And I left you there...
... To die.

But now, nurse, you are climbing back:
A lifeline has been thrown down to you,
And with your determination,
Your iron will to conquer this addiction,
With passion and desire to put behind you this affliction,
You – and you alone – are sticking up two fingers to the wheeler-dealers,
Putting back in place,
Your head,
Your mind,
Your dignity.

You – and you alone, nurse – are stepping out into the sunshine of a new day.
A day where you will find that people smile...
People dance and people sing... and people play...

A day where flowers blossom on a grassy bank,
Where bees drone lazily upon their way from bud to bud.
Where the whole of creation sits, awaiting to join you.

And you WILL do it.

By your effervescent will and sheer determination to succeed.
You will regain your life.
You will wear flowers in your hair.
You will smile like you've never done before.

And, when that day arrives, as it surely will,
We will be here, nurse, to put our arms around you
And kiss you on the cheek...
... To cheer and clap and dance.

For you will be reborn afresh,
Life for you will start again.
Good luck, nurse and God bless.

July 2001

This piece came about when I met a young woman, in an addiction centre, who was a nurse by day and a heron addict by night. She had been balancing the two aspects of her life for many years and had managed to conceal her addiction from her employer and those around her. Eventually she was forced to seek help, for if she had not done so, she knew she would have died prematurely. I could not get my head around the fact that this young woman could be seen as a respectable carer by day and a demon by night!

Jesus Is Alive Today

Jesus is alive today,
Eternal life, He is 'The Way';
Scourged, tortured, put to death,
Ultimate sacrifice, nothing left.
Son of man, hung from a tree,
In death, in life, showed dignity.
Spirit lost, yet spirit found;
All humankind in Him is bound.
Living as in human frame,
In God He lived, from God He came.
Vilified, ridiculed, He gave His life, His all.
Evil sinners vanquished, at His knee did fall.
Twelve apostles, plucked from obscurity,
One betrayed kiss, lost His security.
Do you see Christ? Take in His peace.
All around, including this piece.
Yes, Jesus is alive today.

---

*Can the reader find Jesus here? If so, well done If not, keep searching!!**

*   Answer: The first letter of each line spells out 'Jesus is alive today'!

124

You Are the Salt of the Earth

By the secret of a 'Safe Key',
You enter by stealth...
Having already cared for two.
You are the salt of the earth,
Greeted by a friendly bark:
Ben's affection, instinctive love.
So, what faces you here?
Challenges unknown.
Automatically, you transform from
Partner, daughter, mother, friend...
All left at home, for now, you metamorphose
To a saint.
Respect, smiles, perhaps hidden anxiety.
You are the salt of the earth.*
Routine, preparation, compassion,
Whilst the usual banter emerges.
A tired figure sits before you, still gasping for breath...
Still pushing the boundaries of living.
You allow me to do what I can...
Your pity wells up, inward tears...
You are the salt of the earth.
With emotions hidden, you carry on.
Is it Friday? Hair-wash day!
You wash my back for the 10,000th time :
Coal miner filthy!! But I can't see it anyway!
Trousers removed with professional dignity,
Oversized pyjamas quickly put on.
'Lifeline' secured.
The slip-ons slip off, whilst slippers slip on.
I return to base armchair.
You are the salt of the earth .
Conversation, on my terms.
A mug of tea, made unconsciously.
Write the report – a legal document.

*   Mt 5/13

So, a soothing smile, a gentle touch,
You quietly fade away, by that 'Safe Key'.
"See you soon, my lovely!!"
You are the salt of the earth.

To have carers come into your home three times a day is an intrusion, however 'well behaved' they are. Each carer has their own way of doing things, with the same result in the end. I give my sincere thanks to everyone of my carers over the years. I never previously realised the love and dedication that you give every day. Thank you.

Poor Pretty Puffins

Poor pretty Puffins perform passionately.
Persecuted puffins prance prettily past Peter's place.
Passionate puffins play purposefully, peacefully, persuasively.
Precocious puffins produce precocious puffins.
Prancing puffins pervade private parts!!
Preening puffins puff past potters producing pretty pots.
Parliamentarian puffins pass Prince Philip, parked past plastic palace.
Powerful puffins, perhaps, produce proper preening prodigies.
Pink puffins pull pit ponies past plum plants.
Purple puffins place postcards permanently past Polly's puppy – Peanut!
Peruvian puffins peck parrots' passports – pulverised pieces.
Playful puffins patronise prehistoric, protected penguins.
Pure puffins paint poppies, proudly producing profitable pictures.
Peaceful puffins preen properly, proudly presenting paper peacocks.
Patronising puffins play playfully, planning planet's purpose.

Quiet! Be Still...

I am on the quay
Three hundred years it has stood here...
The wind is howling all around,
White horse waves 'crash'.
Above, grey clouds dash the sky
Their journey never ending.
Rain lashes my face;
Hands, gloveless, freeze.
Fingers numb. I stamp my feet,
Still relentlessly cold.
On the horizon,
Maybe twenty miles off...
A black spot!
No, wrong, it has disappeared.
Illusion – a plank in my eye, perhaps!
A dog bounds up,
Smiling a dog smile.
Drenched brown coat, soaked paws.
Wait... something out there has reappeared,
White horses still driving it to land.

No, gone again...
God, I could do with a mug of tea!
Wait, in sight again...
It's *not* a plank in my eye. No,
It's a boat, a fishing boat.
Tossed up, thrown down,
Sea, as dark as ink.
Dog's ears alert; a bark.
Look, the boat, it's coming this way
The solitary sail, billows...
... Driving homeward.
I can see a lone man on deck
"Ahoy there, over here"...
And another.
They look wet, bedraggled!
Men hauling in huge, but empty nets
They look worn, tired,
"Ahoy"...
The boat, nearing its mooring now
Look, the sea, it's calming;
Grey clouds, turning white.
A bark from the dog, smiles again.
Wagging tail in delight.
O, blue sky above.
Look, the sun is shining on distant hills,
The single sail, brought down
In uniform formation.
A splash from the anchor...
Howling wind... ceases
The clouds sail across the sky
Men, rushing, dashing.
Tasks to complete before debarkation.
Must leave it shipshape!
Here they come now...
The crew are finally coming ashore
"Welcome."
"Ah, lovely dog... hello, boy."
"An horrendous storm out there!"
"Aye, we nearly lost it!"
"I am James, by the way, this is my brother John."
"This is Andrew."

"And this is Peter.
We call him Peter the scruff!!"
"Hi everyone and welcome."
"And who is that? That guy still aboard!!"
"Er... that is The Lord."
"The Lord?"...
"Yes, The Messiah."
"Who?"
"Jesus of Nazareth!!"
"He slept through the storm,
But still calmed it."
He is coming ashore now.
"Jesus, welcome."
A glance to the fishermen...
"Why are you so afraid?
Do you still have no Faith?"
An uncomfortable moment...
We all look at our feet!
"Er... mug of tea, Jesus?"
"That would be nice – no sugar!"

A storm at sea can be terrifying. The storms of life can also be terrifying. The way to survive both is through prayer and a mug of tea – no sugar.

February 2020

Not Worth Reading!!

Some are not the best
Others don't pass the test.
Some, may just, stand the test of time.
There are those which are far too long, like this line.
Some are short.
Long words are often fraught,
Mis-spelt and...
Underlined in Red.
Change them, or I'll be dead,
Though I have to say,
Some may live another day.
Truthful, gritty,
Some are witty but
I just want to hide away
And not return until next Friday.
Of some I am rather proud
But most are demonstrably loud:
They make me feel like an utter fraud.
In my heart I could easily thrust a sword.
So, what is next?
I don't know
Until ten tons of peas fall on my toe!
It could be good, it could be bad.
If that's the case, it will make me really sad.
Well, that is my life,
A total sacrifice,
A loser from beginning to end,
Like this poem, which I can't mend!

July 2020

Fingers for Life...

Look at these fingers now,
Long, spindle-like, bent.
No longer able to control a pen...
Or grip a knife, fork and spoon.
Just look at them now – dead!

Once, when just two hours old
These same fingers,
Searched out a mother's breast.
Felt the tenderness, the warmth...
These fingers grasped, as life-nourishing milk
Slipped from mother to child.
Natural, uncompromising, pure.

In time, these same fingers learnt
To pick up sticky food.
They were the lifeline for a hungry body
But society dictates we all learn to use cutlery!
So, to be ambidextrous is essential.
Cutting a sausage is a challenge!
Gravy with a fork – impossible!

At school the fingers learn new skills
Holding, pencil, crayon, paintbrush.
Colours of the paint are inviting...
Red, Yellow, Blue and Green.
Fingers of the Rainbow!
'Smack' onto paper. Fingers imprint in...
Red, Yellow, Blue and Green.
What fun!!

These same fingers grow at a steady pace...
Squish into clay, dance into plasticine,
Mud pies in the garden, but best of all...
Wet sand sticks like glue... on a sun-kissed beach.
Dry sand falls away like powder, such fun.
Cold fingers, wet fingers, numb fingers,
Clean fingers, dirty fingers.

Then... without warning... one cut finger.
Blood gushes forth... red spots fall to the floor.
"Hold it under the cold tap."...
Bandage...
Wrapped tightly to keep the blood inside!
"Does it hurt? Be brave, my little soldier!"
Two days later, bandage off.
A proud scar to show off to mates...
"Cor..." "Look at that!"

From boyhood to manhood in an instant,
Those same dainty fingers turn into tools for life,
Controlling a spade, planting cabbages,
Wheeling a hammer, screwdriver and drill.
Fixing a fence, a leaking pipe, building a wall.
Grasping a pint, throwing a dart,
Defending a wicket. True, fingers for life.
Changing the oil on the car now
These same fingers, black, grime-entrenched,
Black nails, never to become clean again.

Suddenly, fortunes change...
A gold ring is lovingly placed on one finger
For life...
These same fingers are asked, once again,
To caress, to be warm, tender and erotic.
They respond to love.
Demand now, to be clean with manicured nails.
Shake hands with a prince... polite conversation.

But, for these same fingers, the task is not done.
Grasp tightly a new life, just two hours old.
"Hold her head, don't hold her so tightly!"
Then, a revelation... see,
Those fingers that have been through the mill...
Are holding the tiny fingers of another...
Another life... another beginning.
And, once again, fingers search out... for life.

So, look again at these fingers,
long, spindle-like, bent
Remember the life they have lived.
The tasks they have been forced to do.
The service they have been forced to give
The injuries they have endured!
All, without reprisal or complaint.
So, in a quiet moment...
Look... and give thanks.
Thank You.

February 2020

Don't Touch Me...

Hands withered, transparent, ghostly,
Purple veins protrude like poisonous snakes
Slithering aimlessly to dead fingers.
Thin, once energetic thumbs, now arthritically bent.
Long, yellowing nails in need of attention.
Cuticles, no longer a pride and joy,
Have all but disappeared by neglect.
Don't touch me...

Don't touch me...
Arms, once as strong as steel girders...
Now, withered to kidney-bean sticks.
Shallow skin hangs off them, like the carcass of a deer.
Wrinkled and limp – dead white flesh – unwanted now.
That old tattoo of a roaring lion, put there fifty-two years ago,
Pride... to impress and it did its job,
But now, it is a dead old cat, all nine lives – lived.
Don't touch me...

Don't touch me...
A chest, once as golden as a sunset in paradise
Six-pack, the envy of the entire universe...
Now, the sun has finally set.
The chest has shrunk to half a pack!
While sullen skin has turned Snow White ...
... Without dwarfs.
Who wants to see that same chest now? No one...
Don't touch me...

Don't touch me...
Thighs and calves were strong and rigid,
Walking a thousand miles or more.
Now, they shuffle from room to room,
Zimmer as a companion.
The leg muscles are tired and worn,
Can support this frail frame – no more.
Knees crack with the thought of rest...
Don't touch me...

Don't touch me...
Toes, hidden from the world, no longer move.
Feet, purple, starved of light for so many years.
Hardened skin still taking the knocks;
Brogues are yesterday's news.
Only slippers shuffle on lino now!
So, look... by not looking.
See, by not seeing.
But that fit figure is still here – but it's gone.
Don't touch me...

February 2020

This is a chilling piece about old age and frailty. When young, we are proud of our bodies, in order to attract. When elderly, we hide our bodies away through embarrassment... but we are still there, inside, locked in!!

"I Have Seen Your Future"

You matter so much to me... please believe me.
I will forever be by your side.
I know you are apprehensive... frightened, even.
Come, sit with me and tell me how you feel.
The death of our bodies is part of our life together.
But come, you must trust me.
Our unseen soul never dies,
Our earthly bodies are only half the story.
They are given to us, in whatever form,
As a 'Gift from God',
A gift to care for... and to cherish.
As we pass through life, we all...
... Come to realise our bodies will not last forever,
Just a lifetime...
But I have seen your future:
"I am you future."
At the time of my choosing... come
I will take you by the hand... and
Lead you to the door of your Eternal Life...
That door will open and we will, together, step through.
And there, you will be – that unseen soul –
In the gentleness of your Eternal Life,
A Life, where nothing will harm you,
A Life, where peace, calmness and solemnly will hold you,
A Life, where you can smile and laugh again,
A Life where you can lie on the bed of compassion.
Come, sit with me and tell me how you feel... now.
Yes, you matter so much to me.
I will, forever be by your side... your disciple... in death.

June 2020

So often, death is portrayed as being a sad event. True, we are hidden from our loved ones, but what Christ promised us, surely, must outweigh our loss. John 4:13-14: Jesus said to her, "Everyone who drinks of this water will be thirsty again, but whoever drinks of the water that I will give him will never be thirsty again, The water that I will give him will become in him a spring of water welling up to eternal life."

(Chicken) Pie in the Sky...

As I was eating chicken pie,
I saw a chicken in the sky!
A beady stare she gave to me:
"What are you eating for your tea?"
I looked down at my plate.
"Chicken pie," I did relate!
"That is my mother," the chicken said,
"Breast, legs, thigh and head!"
Poor young chicken in the sky,
A lonely orphan, flying by.
"Come," I said, "And be my mate.
Fly down here, sit on my plate."
But that chicken knew my game;
She didn't want to die the same.
"No," she said in a chicken's voice,
"I'll take my chance under that Rolls Royce."
So that young chicken took to the sky
And didn't end up in my chicken pie... Today!!

January 2020

I Am in the Box Again...

I am in the box again.
It's dark and dank inside.
The floor is high, the roof is low,
The walls coincide.
There is a window with a net,
No one can see inside.
It's above the level I can see out:
What is the good of that?
People pass by,
And glance in the box,
But they see nothing,
For it is invisible.
They hear my screams,
They hear my shouts and wonder where I am,
But they see no one.
Looking out of the netted window,
I see matchstick images of passers-by,
Un-noticed, unseeing,
With visual disregard.
It is not all gloom, doom,
Not all stark, dark,
For in here, I am safe,
Cocooned, as would be a foetus.
For, in here, no one can see me.
They cannot see me hurting,
Bursting, waiting,
Dying.
Sometimes, but only sometimes,
Some careful soul
Taps upon the window pane
And peers through the net.
They smile,
Even dangle the key in front of me,
Give a cheesy grin
From behind the glass.
At times like these I feel apprehensive,
even scared of what may be... out there.
So, I politely say, "No thanks,
Please go and throw the key away."

And that leaves me here
Where I was before,
At the start.
I am in the box again.

I wrote this piece at a particularly low time in my life. I was re-adjusting to living alone, whilst still having to maintain the routine of holding down a job. My isolation was made all the more intense because no one around me appeared to acknowledge my distress... no one spoke of my situation!

When I Came into Jail...

When I came into jail, I left Jesus at the gate.
I am tough and mean and angry and I don't need Him as me mate.
I know how to handle things,
I can do some 'arm... in a really nasty way...
Re-arrange a face, break a leg, slash a throat...
If you see me comin' it's best to run away.

When I came into jail, I left Jesus at the gate
I'll serve my time... bugger-off, just leave me to me fate
I don't want no Chaplain comin' in to gloat...
... Don't want no religion pushed right down me' throat
Just leave me be... go away... go and save some other bloody soul.

When I came into jail, I left Jesus at the gate.
I was banged-up with Terry, who *said* he was a mate...
Terry's there for life, but he never said what 'e had done...!!
But I can guess... 'cos he's a mess... reading his bible every day!
Saying prayers, with rosary beads, and claiming Jesus is The Way...
Huh!

When I came into jail, I left Jesus at the gate.
Terry invited me to Church... I laughed ... "Why, do you want more money on the plate?"
"Keep your God," I screamed... "I left him at the gate.

My life's already in the shit... I've been flushed right down the pan... for me it's
too bloody late.
God can't reach me now for I am a condemned man."...
... So Terry went to church alone and I sat in me pad and cried.
Wished that I had not been born; I'd wished that I had died.

When I came into jail, I left Jesus at the gate.
A screw came round me cell, said Terry had met his fate.
He was fighting for his life... and may not make it through the night.
I sat alone for hours, missing Terry's words...
... Just looking at his bible, his prayer book and his beads.
The Chaplain came at 6am... told me Terry'd died,
One single stab wound to the neck – he couldn't have survived.

When I came into jail, I left Jesus at the gate.
I couldn't understand why Terry 'ad always been me mate.
Well, I treated him so rotten, told him to commit suicide
I used pages from 'is bible to make meself a spliff
But he never did give up on me... he was always by my side.

When I came into jail, I left Jesus at the gate.
I can't believe I am sayin' this... but now, I need him as me mate.
"Come to church," the chaplain said, " to remember Terry's last few days."
"What, me? A sadistic, violent slob like me!!"
"Yes," he said, "we all come to Christ in different ways."

When I came into jail, I left Jesus at the gate.
I went to church, for after all, Terry 'ad been me mate!
Saw the Cross of Jesus and... someone smiled at me,
A guy I used to hate – put his arms around me – "Welcome, mate."
I listened to the silence, and thought of who I'd been,
I felt alone and lost and empty... my life was so obscene.
It was then I wished I never had left Jesus at the gate.
I want Him back – as a true and lovin' mate

When I came into jail, I didn't know Jesus was God's only Son
Back in me cell, I wept – and remembered what I'd done.
The times I'd kicked a head in – and laughed every single time.
And now – what had I got to show, for all that sickening crime?
Four prison walls, and addicted to that *fucking* crack cocaine.

When I came into jail, I left Jesus at the gate.
I got down on me knees that night and through my pain and tears
I said that I was sorry and asked... "God, please take away my fears."
I went back to church and told 'im what I'd done...
"Well done, my boy," the chaplain said, "you *are* redeemed, my son."

When I came out of jail, I found Jesus – waiting at the gate...
He put his arms around me and I said 'good-bye' to hate.
He led me to a better life – one I did not know
... With love, gratitude, compassion, from Him these things do flow.

Jail is but a memory now, as beside Jesus I still walk...
He guides my every step, and through prayer we – talk the talk.
I met a woman, we had a babe – and now I've seen 'The Light',
I got a job in youth work, showing kids how *not* to fight...
I feel so much different now... the old me don't exist.
I look upon my fellow man as a friend, with whom I *can* co-exist.
Now, I really love The Lord, He's been my saving grace...
Now, I have a future, with a smile upon me face!!

May 2017

Whilst having never served a prison term myself, I have met many young men who have. This piece is based upon a collection of individuals I have had the privilege to meet – in prison. I have morphed them into one angry and violent young man!

I Saw Jesus the Other Day

I saw Jesus the other day on a hospital ward.
Sitting, silently, by the bed of an elderly woman.
The silence, was deafening, as later that evening, she died.
Her family were terribly upset...
Their mother, sister, grandmother, aunt and great aunt had been taken from them.
But, Jesus simply sat there... in the silence... in the grief.

I saw Jesus the other day... in a prison cell.
The prisoner had committed a terrible crime,
Rape.
He had already served eight years.
He had another four to go.
Jesus was saying that he couldn't change the past...
But maybe the future *could* be different.
"As far as he was concerned, he'll always be here... it's up to you," He said!

I saw Jesus the other day. He was in our local supermarket.
He was just reaching for a tin of macaroni cheese from the top
Shelf... and handing it to a young man in a wheel-chair.
He put the tin in the young man's basket...
The man's hands were deformed, and his face disfigured.
I lost sight of Jesus after that... He simply disappeared into the crowd.

I saw Jesus the other day. It was in church.
Surprisingly, I had not seen Him in church before!
The priest was holding up the bread and the wine.
"This is My body – given for you."
"This is My blood – shed for you."
I was confused!
How could Jesus give *ME* his body and his blood?
Then I remembered.
I had seen Him – when I had least expected it...
...And He had given-up everything for me,
Jesus had hung on the cross – and died... for me... and for all of us.
He had been at the bedside, in the prison cell, in the supermarket... and in church – for us!

Jesus lives in ordinary people... everyday people... good people of my community.
So, Father God, let my eyes be open, let my ears hear.
Open my mind, so I may *see* Jesus in the everyday...
And when I do see Him, let me give thanks for His love, His compassion,
His faithfulness which lives within me... and within each one of us.

No comment on this one... you decide.

Travels of a Young Woman!!

Now, there was this woman from Wolverhampton
Who stepped off a train in Northampton.
She stayed in a 'Premier Inn'
Where she committed a terrible sin!!
She then boarded a train to Skegness
But once there, thought she'd reached Loch Ness.
She searched for the mythical monster
But only found one singular lobster.
With that she hired a jet plane
And flew all the way to the Ukraine.
Once there, she flopped on the bed
Shattered, with thoughts in her head.
Next morning, she fancied a fella
Went up to him, and called herself Bella.
He got wind of her game
And thought the same,
So decided to call himself Stan.
But Bella was wary, of this gorgeous man,
So she lured him into her bed,
Pulled off his shirt, and said:
"Are you sure you're a man?"
"No," he replied, "I am a woman called Stan!"
Without further ado, she jumped on a boat;
It was so small, it could hardly keep afloat!
During the voyage, she spoke to the Captain,
Who told her he was very good at actin'.
She believed him, of course,
And told him she was in the police force!!
Once in Southampton,
She bought a train ticket to Wolverhampton.
And there she went into a shop to buy a huge toy
Which she gave to her beautiful, three-year-old boy.
So what became of that woman from Wolverhampton...?
... Nothing, but she was happy!!

Lichfield, March 2020

The Donkey and the Poppy

The donkey and the poppy stand in the potter's field
Donkey carries Virgin, fruit of her womb to yield.
Poppy waits for Christ's blood to paint her petals red.
As three hundred thousand solders to Passion-dale are led.

Donkey is the first to see the manger's Holy Child,
He kneels before the Saviour, solemn, meek and mild.
Poppy lifts her blackened face to warn the boys so young,
But all in vain, it is too late, the 'Last Post' has been sung.

Donkey flees the massacre of every male infant child,
He saves the Son of God, as Herod is reviled.
Poppy waits and watches as the boys dig in.
Postcard back to Blighty, "Dear Mum," waiting for the party to begin.

Donkey is then ridiculed, scorned and spat upon,
As Jesus Christ is given to us: "This is my precious Son."
Poppy drops her seeds around, in preparation for the kill.
Sons and lovers, fathers, brothers, wait for death's cold chill.

Donkey, tethered to a post, awaits his Master's voice.
"Untie the colt and bring to Me, let the crowds rejoice."

Poppy bows her head in grief, she knows her fate is sealed.
Men have died, boys are slain, in the killing-field.

Donkey carries the King of Kings through the city streets.
Shouts above, palms beneath, the happy throng He meets.
Poppy seeds lie desolate, in a field of bloody mud
Eerie silence, the smell of death, in the swelling flood.

Donkey watches as Christ stumbles, cross upon his back.
A tear shed, a moment lost, the crowd turned to a pack.
Poppy's blood-red petals fall, as do men and boys,
Lives snuffed out, simply gone, no future they'll enjoy.

Donkey, he now has the cross, given to him to wear.
As Christ is hung from a tree, our sins He promises to bear.
Poppy waits in that cold, dark, dank, desolate place,
"Goodnight boys," as she wipes a tear from her blackened face.

So, donkey's task is done, save the final deadly game,
A symbol of humility, compassion and reframe.
Poppy's task has just begun, for, in the Flanders field,
She sways upon the western wind, a symbol for lives that yield.

Through the years and centuries donkey and poppy wait.
For that very moment when history concludes their fate.
For now, they are both symbols, 'Beast of burden', 'Flower of the dead'.
And by Christ's own crucifixion, all humanity is fed.

So let us all give thanks for the beast and flower.
And in them see the love of God, each second, minute, hour.
For, as Christ stretched out His arms, and for us He died,
Donkey hung his head, and poppy simply cried.

2019

This was swirling around my head for ages before I wrote it down. The horror of the crucifixion linked with the modern horror of World War One, cannot, in my view, be separated by the passage of the centuries. The 'symbols', i.e. The donkey & the poppy represent me/us as onlookers to these two tragic events.

From the year 2014 to 2018 in Lichfield Cathedral, a single candle was lit in one of the side chapels. It was there to remind us of the many millions who had died in the Great War, just 100 years earlier. I often used to go into the chapel and just sit and ponder the significance of the candle, which was never extinguished in the four years.

Since childhood, my favourite animal has been the donkey. I have always liked the gentleness and the loyalty of the Beast. I have admired its strength and its willingness to please. Most of all, I have loved the fact that donkeys have a distinguished cross on their backs... the cross of Christ given to them, so the story goes, by Jesus himself, for carrying him triumphantly into Jerusalem on that first Psalm Sunday.

... And my favourite flower... well, you've probably guessed. Yes, the poppy. There is no finer sight than a host of bright red poppies blowing in the wind in a field of corn.

Scott Free, a Friend Like You...

Dearest Scott, it's great to have a friend like you,
I really do appreciate you being around.
I love the way you treat me,
Always so thoughtful, so sensitive, so respectfully.
I admire your intelligence and your inner strength,
And you really are so kind to me.
You are so compassionate, always thinking of others before yourself.
I love your soul, your mind, your very being.
You have been so successful in your career
Reaching the top of your game,
Never exploiting the poor, always helping the vulnerable and the weak.
I admire your sense of seriousness, yet you can be such fun.
Your heartfelt love for others and so generous in spirit, towards me...
... And all whom you meet.
You light up any room.
Oh yes, it's great to have you as a friend,
No, please don't say a word,
Or whisper in my ear in that way,
Just accept the praise – without embarrassment.
No please, don't touch me there
Or run your fingers through my hair
Or gaze at me in that peculiar way
Please don't laugh at what I say.
Why stand so close?
Why undo the buttons of my blouse?
Don't run your fingers down my leg
People may be watching us – I beg.
No, please don't hold me so very tight
Or clasp your hand over my mouth,
That is just not right!
Careful, this skirt is new, don't try to rip it in that way
Oh, you are hurting me with your grip.
I implore you, come no closer
Oh no, don't touch me there – I beg
I have to go now, Agggh – don't grasp my wrists!
Please, I will be late, I cannot stay.
Please don't be so rough with me, I pray.
Please, don't go on with this foolish prank,
Oh no, not my tights.

I am too weak to resist your advance.
No, please don't do anything we may both regret.
No, I am frightened now – please stop this madness.
I trusted you with my life,
I will not submit without a fight.
O God, no, please, not that,
I am not ready or willing to allow you to...
No, God you are hurting me, more than I can bear.
Limb from limb from
Very limb are being wrenched in two.
Please, listen to me, this is wrong!!
No, no, no,
I cannot breathe, your weight is crushing my ribs.
My legs are being torn from my body.
O God,
Please – I beg you – *stop!*
My heart now also is wrenched in two: I have been invaded.
My life has changed till death .

(SILENCE – *for 15 seconds*)
(*In rage:*)
Go away. Please, allow me some space, at least...
I cannot see, everything is blurred, God what have I done?
I am confused, my body aches from outside in!
My skirt is bloodstained now and torn beyond repair.
Just go, leave me alone, I have done my worst.
No, it's OK, I'll get a taxi home.
Perhaps I'll get my dad to pick me up,
No, I shan't tell anyone – yes, I know you have your reputation to consider.
You never want to see me again, I understand!
I am the most despicable monster that walks the earth...
I just want to go now – and have a bath.
Forget it ever happened, leave me here.
Wait, before you go, help me to my feet.
Pass me my handbag,
My shoes, pass them to me please,
Oh, my tights are torn...
Yes, I admit, I am just a stupid woman
Who egged you on and 'asked for it'...
I realise now, that I was wrong!
I know that is just the way it is.

151

I am so sorry I put you in that situation.
No, I should have not worn this blouse tonight,
Yes, it is far too tight.
Yes, this skirt is too short as well... I see that now!
Please forgive my behaviour.
Good night, Scott.

August 2017

This piece came from the very depth of my imagination. I hope, perhaps, it conveys for the reader, the trauma of rape and the tremendous hurt done by a man – to a woman, physically, emotionally as well as spiritually. The experience ALWAYS leaves her with a lifetime of blame and self recrimination!! Whilst he appears to get off... Scott Free.

From Birth Pangs to Death

(The Broken Poppy)

I found you broken at the door of death,
Raised you and thought about your beauty – lost.
Gave you the tears of Christ and prayed you would live again.
I waited. Like waiting for a chrysalis to break,
To reveal not a plain benign mule but a bud of unparalleled ecstasy,
A beauty of which dreams are made in my childhood fantasy...
But before you show yourself, you hang your head on the devil's floor,
Then wait until the moon is aligned with Venus,
As the stars begin to dance in the Creator's hands.
Then, and only then, you move, though I do not see that movement...
... For I am too pre-occupied, filling my head with plans of men.
Busy eating from the forbidden fruit of economic gain too busy to see
you move.
But move you do, breaking the fragile seal of your incarceration
With the delicate twitch of a cat's whisker.
You use the pushing power of some force, known only to God...
But has the power to release, from your prison, using the keys given up by
nature's jailer.
Slow as an Acorn grows to Oak.
Slow as the tide consumes the land you reveal your jewel,
And this is no imitation paste worn by those who strut their stuff on a second
class cat-walk.
No, you are pure.

You are the real, undiluted, genuine gem that I have seen, but once before in a distant memory.

You, you surprise me with your hue, for, not as I believed you would be,
The blood red of fallen heroes.

No, you show yourself in a 'purple' gown!
The purple of Christ's cloak as He awaited trial and execution
Under a crown of thorns.

The purple of the bishopric, the purple of seats on a Virgin train.
And you have your purple, laced with nature's black, to ensure that
The devil's eye still watches.

As you flower to fruition you give the world, a world which cares to see you,
A diamond at your heart, encircled by the shimmer of your stamen –
Bidding new life, when you are gone.

So, you sip the water of life into your very soul and turn your golden face
towards the Light... the Light that did create you, the Light that will
Destroy you.

For two unending days you shine and give pleasure upon a world
That rarely notices lest it sees the pleasure given by your curbside cousin.
But, oh too short a time, for when I speak to you again, you are dead.

The purple gown has been discarded, the ball is over and you have slipped away,
prior to the Midnight Hour.

Your diamond, the glow of life has vanished and given way to nature's pregnant
pod...

... Though, you have not truly died, for there, inside, unseen, is the life that will
live when God chooses to reveal your glory once again, in another time, another
season,
When another Poppy will adorn the world.

The Poppy is my very favourite flower of all time. Either singly or a host of them woven into a field of summer corn, their beauty is unparalleled. Many years ago now, I found a single poppy bud on the floor which had been picked and discarded. I put it in water and over the next three days, just watched as the flower formed, then it died. No one else saw it, but me and it struck me that as a rule, we don't see nature forming, living briefly then dying. Most of us are just too busy to see the wonders of nature on our doorstep.

Stoic, Dependable, Confident

Stoic, dependable, confident, with an air of 'rightness' about you.
I never knew your name
To me you were always Mrs Veysey.
You walked beside me, all my life, as a surrogate mother
Sweet memories of the 1950s
Lady, candy – different as chalk from cheese.
Collecting spiders from your privet hedge,
Eating your Nasturtium leaves... hmm, tasted of pepper.
I saw you with your own mother,
Caring for her as your own daughter has cared for you.
Long summer days of impromptu tea-parties in your garden,
Your never-ending smile, laughter and patience...
... Stoic, dependable, confident, with an air of 'rightness' about you.
From me, and the rest of of the world, your difficulties were hidden.
Ken was kindly, but his childhood had formed the man.
Your first child, a girl, beat me into this world by just thirty-eight days.
You met Joan at the school gate on that first day.
We wore brand new gaberdine macs, with belts.
I wore a cap – a little boy of the 1950s.
Your second child, the gift of a boy – family complete.
... And someone for us to tease, push around.
Colin was the first boy I ever 'bossed about' – and the last.
On the way home from school...
... Collecting spent matches from the gutter!
But perhaps you never knew that! ...
We found a kitten and returned it to old lady Poxon.
At her back-door I was frightened, even though I was a boy.
So scared that she may eat me for her dinner!!
In April 1960 my world fell apart
We moved house, to the other side of the world...
... Well, the other side of the town anyway!!
No more playing with 'Lady'. No more bouncing naked on your couch.
No more meals at your house or playing with rubber Lego bricks,
Or dodging Ken's glances of disapproval.
But contact was not lost altogether... it just became more 'arranged',
... More formal now. No more dipping in and out.
Rolleston Road was 'posh' then.
Panelled walls seemed austere to me, but your loving smile and
Infectious laugh soon made everything OK.

Marion was a girl... I was a boy... at this age, we drifted... but
You did not let my mother down... she needed you to...
Be there, to talk, to share, someone in whom to confine, to cry with,
and engage...
And you listened... you took it all in, you empathised.
Still stoic, dependable, confident, with that air of 'rightness' about you.
Big schools – and Marion drifted from my life, but you made
Connections with Eileen through the Rambling Club...
And you became the third sister that Joan and Eileen
Had lost in childhood...
You said a long goodbye to Ken before you were both ready...
Now you had only yourself to depend upon.
In your own inimitable way,

You re-configured yourself into a single woman,
Stoic, dependable, confident, with an air of 'rightness' about you.
You made yourself available to your community,
And gained respect from far and wide.
You maintained your friendship with Joan,
Who maybe wasn't as strong as she had made out.
Suddenly, grandchildren on your knee,
But you kept up all your interests,
Faithfully and with a quiet compassion for all.
I was now a man – of sorts –
And our relationship became adult and I could call you Barbara
For the first time, though I found it hard.
On rare occasions we would meet in the street...
A razor-sharp memory, you always knew me.
Joan faded from our lives and finally...
From our world, but you were there, to say your farewell to her.
Generations tend to blur and I lost touch
Until, one day, we met at a garden centre,
And when I saw you, all the passions came flooding back.
Walking stick in hand did not diminish the zest for life...
... Stoic, dependable, confident, with an air of 'rightness' about you.
I reminded you of my childhood days
And how you had featured so prominently...
But you dismissed your contribution.
Thanks to modern tech, Marion has kept me in the loop...
Frail, weak, tired, these are not words I recognise...
I do not wish to burst the bubble of my memories.

You will always, always be, for me...
... Stoic, dependable, confident, with an air of 'rightness' about you.
Thank you, Barbara, for being with me my whole life through.

For those who were not there, it is almost impossible to relate the impact Barbara Veysey has had upon both my childhood and adult life. She would deny it, of course, but I know what I know. This piece sums up, in 722 rather pathetic words, 100 years of life of an exceptional woman. Barbara died peacefully, with her family around her, at 12 minutes past midnight on Wednesday 24th January 2019 in her 101st year.
Thank you, Barbara.

Crossroads of Life!

Reaching the crossroads in a busy city...
... Can be a nightmare...
I am alone, confused...Which way? That way...
... Which way shall I go?
This way! That way? Right or Left!
I am not sure? The satnav says straight on!
No, no... it's left at the crossroads. I am confused!
Oops... mind that bike!
Well, which way is it? Right I'll go right,
But... maybe it's left!!
I must concentrate and make up my mind!
Mind that bus...
... I am in the middle lane now...
But I want to turn right!
STOP, no don't, carry on!!
In an unknown city, I reach the crossroads...
... Choices to be made, in an instant...
Straight on, left, right or return!
The satnav is my only directional angel – now.

Reaching the crossroads in a busy life...
... Can be a nightmare
I am alone, confused... Which way? That way...
... Which way shall I go?
This way! That way? Right or left!
I am not sure. No satnav to help me now!
No, no, it's left at the crossroads of life!
Oops... mind that temptress!
Well, which way is it?
Right... I'll go right, but it is desolate and lonely.
But ... maybe it's left, unknown, frightening and forlorn.
I must concentrate and make up my mind – my decision alone.
Mind that emotional blackmail!
... I am in middle age now, the way is still uncertain
But I am turning right!
STOP, no don't, carry on!!

In an unknown life, I reach the crossroads...
... Choices to be made, but, perhaps time to reflect.
Straight on, left, right or return!
Jesus my satnav now!

March 2020

When Did It Happen? I Missed It!

A blue-tipped butterfly lands on a blade of grass,
As a dragonfly hovers over running water.
An eagle glides on a current of air,
While a badger gives birth in her set.

The 6.45 to Euston makes up for the time it has lost,
As roads are swept early morning before sunrise.
Milk is delivered pre-dawn, unseen,
While the newspaper lad does his round before school.

The disease enters the body by stealth...
And sits dormant for a year or more.
Eventually as slowly as acorn turns to oak, it rises
While I carry on, unaware, much as before.

The doctor is baffled and recommends pills.
The Oncologist undertakes tests, but draws a blank.
The Neurologist examines the evidence,
While I wait for the news, I don't want to hear.

In the laboratory, other conditions are carefully dismissed,
A conclusion is reached – beyond doubt.
The medics confer and enter statistics on-line,
While the diagnosis is explained amidst tears and sorrow.

I continue my life, as though nothing is wrong...
And make light of the pain, I still carry on.
I laugh at the prospect of the life changing condition,
While everyone offers their time and their talents.

Suddenly... things change for the worse as the breathing slows
Four falls in a fortnight make me aware.
The legs don't react to the brain's instructions,
While the rest of the body is not getting the message.

999, blue light, rush, dash, out of my way!!
"I am your Consultant, we'll get to the bottom of this."
"I am your nurse from the Philippines, I am here for you."
While I lie alone in a hospital bed, thinking of life and of death.

"Hmm, clot on the lung, that is not good,
But we'll soon have you home, as we need the bed."
"I am a Physio, named Hayley.,...I'll do what I can,"
While others outside wait, worry, cry and console.

"Don't ever climb stairs, so sleep in the lounge
Try holding your head up high, use the PEG for fluid and food.
Use this Zimmer to help you with walking,"
While the world passes me by!

Three carers a day to help wash and put on a shirt.
They talk of *their* lives – and not mine!
They are kindness itself in the face of unparalleled gloom
While the world gets on with its life – without me.

So, a blue-tipped butterfly continues to land on a blade of grass,
As a dragonfly still hovers over running water.
An eagle continues to glide on a current of air,
While a badger gives birth in her set... once again.
But I missed it!!

November 2019

My "If"

IF you can keep on barking when all about you
Don't hear the door-bell and blame you for making such a noise,
If you can trust yourself with a biscuit when others doubt you can!
But make that biscuit last just half a second;
If you can wait for a walk and not be tired of waiting
Or being told you're going then you don't,
Or being told you are a nuisance, when you're not
And yet you still lie down at your master's feet:

If you can sleep all night and all the day as well,
If you can sleep next to Master all night long,
If you can wake at 5.30am and wait patiently till six,
Then treat your mistress to a walk in the early morning mist,
If you can wait to do your business on the grassy bank,
Where Mistress cannot reach it with a doggie bag,
So as she struggles, you just wait for a disaster,
Then stoop and decide to do a second load,
If you can make two heaps, when one would do,
And then turn your back, as if it was not you.
Then run, pulling Mistress over in the dark,
And never admit that it was you, "Oh sorry, Miss!"
If you can force your legs to keep on running,
Then swerve, to look back and see if she is OK!
And tarry a while, till she catches up with you,
And don't ignore her cries of "Hold on!"

If you can walk in crowds and keep to heel on the lead,
Or walk with Robin, on those long, long walks you love.
If you can talk to other dogs in a friendly way,
And other hounds sniff you where they shouldn't,
If you can accept their advances, without alarm
With sixty seconds limited to sniffing time.
Yours, is the earth to roll in and everything that's in it
And – what is more – you'll be a black Labrador, my SON!
... And we love you, just the same!!

30th December 2019

Many people have written their own version of Rudyard Kipling's poem, "IF".
This is my version – hot off the press.

Mighty Natural Disaster... or MND!

Don't talk to me of disasters, happening all around,
I will ignore the negative stuff – how does that bloody sound?
Don't tell me this is real or this is how it *has* to be,
Just don't be so down-hearted when it comes to 'Mr Me'.

Yes, I have had my bad times and done things that I should not,
But this is no retribution, or some well-conceived, untimely plot.
Is this not someone wagging a finger at me,
Saying, "You naughty boy... you should have let it be!!"?

OK, I have lived my life the only way I know how...
Smiling, joking, not living for the future, but for the here and now.
I have not cheated anyone out of what was rightly theirs,
I have not sneered at anyone or stolen stocks 'n' shares.

I have not even taken a woman who didn't belong to me,
Though, yes, the temptation was there for everyone to see!!
OK, I can't say I've lived a Godly life; I know I've been no saint,
But a downright rogue, hypocrite, scrounger, I definitely ain't!

You can chastise me all you like, but say it to my face,
For it won't make no difference, I'll still be in disgrace.
I have to say, I never saw it looming, or coming up behind.
I never even realised my life would be re-aligned.

Yeah, I should seen it, creeping up on me.
Looking back in hindsight, signs *were* there for me to see.
But when life is so hectic, you tend to ignore the important things,
And concentrate on the flippant and the annoying little 'Blings'.

I realise I am not the only one, that I am not alone,
But that does not really help – but I know I should not moan!!
Trying to keep positive is what I have always done,
Now it is even more important to show that I am having fun.

I think it's funny, when my legs don't move as I want them too,
I feel that I should run, but I can't make it to the loo!!
The staircase defeats me it is like having Everest in my home.
I even struggle to do my hair with a brush and comb!

Using the zimmer can cause a problem too,
But in that bloody wheelchair, just see what I can do.
Ran into the local vicar, just the other day,
He said, "God bless you son, I suppose for you I'll have to pray!!"

In the chair, I zoom around at some amazing speed,
The other day, the doctor came and thought I was on 'the weed'!
OK, I know there is a serious side to this thing called MND,
I know I have to act all serious when the doctor looks at me.

"Where does it hurt, where is the pain?
Are you really serious when you say, you want to parachute from a plane?"
"Come on, Doc, you know me better than that,
With this MND, all I want to do is die, before I get too bloody fat!"

"I was 10 stone 4, now I am 9 stone 6.
You must have some tablets, with which this body you can fix!!
Yes, I know about the legal side, and giving my consent.
When someone else decides to switch me off, even though it's kindly meant."

Yes, I realise I won't live till I am 97,
But before I knock on those holy gates of Heaven,
It would be nice to see my grandkids prosper,
And I would love to see my daughter, as years ago... I lost her!

So, thank you God – if you're really there!!
... For giving me this time, which has been reasonably fair.
And as I make my way the Heaven to be by Jesus's side,
I will be as good as gold and will enjoy the ride.

So you don't need to worry 'bout me no more,
I'll just sit here with Him, waiting by this open door.
And when you appear at the pearly gates
We can embrace and kiss and vow to be eternal mates!!

February 2020

Well... I Can Only Dream, Now!

I am sitting on a log on a deserted beach.
The golden sand stretches as far as the eye can see in both directions.
Behind the sand line, palm trees sway in the gentle, warm breeze.
In front of me is a turquoise sea.
White-horse waves lap the sand in the motion of a never-ending rhythm,
Over and over and over again...
A solitary gull soars above me in a cloudless sky.
I look, to where sea and sky meet on the horizon...
The colours merge, one with the other... blues, yellows and vivid orange of a
sunrise.
I dream wistfully, of the day ahead... sand, sea and sky and maybe a cold beer!
Suddenly, there is a noise behind me and out of the palm trees appears, a very
bouncy black Labrador.
He races up to me, smiles and gives a loud 'bark'... as if to say, "Come on, let's go
swimming!"
Then, at the speed of light, he dashes over the sand and bounds into the sea.
Submerged up to his neck, he barks again, "Come on!!"
I walk, barefoot, down to the water's edge. The warm sea laps my toes until
eventually, my ankles are covered.
The dog is some way off by now.
"Come back!" I shout.
He barks again and begins the long voyage back to shore.

I anticipate his next move, as all dog-lovers do! as he bounds up to me and licks my face.

Yes, just one foot away from me, in prehistoric and ancient tradition, he draws all his strength... and shakes.

Lashings of water cover me from head to foot.

The sea continues to lap the shore, as we amble back up to the log.

The dog turns around twice, as did his ancestors, then he lies down and, within ten seconds, appears to be asleep.

So, here am I... sitting in my armchair in Middle England.

Eyes closed, dog at my feet, listening to the waves lapping the shore... on CD... and in my imagination.

February 2020

Life Is Fragile...

Life is fragile
No more so than, in an unexpected moment, when...
...A trampled, flightless bird enters our urban world.
Blackbird, thrush, sparrow or starling?
I don't know, I care even less.
All know is, she has been robbed of her natural instinct.
Oh so tenderly, I hold this delicate, broken body...
...In my cupped hands, to recreate her nest. I can feel her tiny bones,
Hear her softly beating heart, for the final time on Earth.
The warmth of her body, her downy feathers.
I re-align my own self, as...
...Compassion wells up inside of me!
Two brown eyes – look into mine...
Tears... are they mine or hers?
Is that a tentative smile upon her beak?
The left wings drags, lifeless.
What a dilemma –
This defenceless creature is now reliant upon me.
She moves between my fingers...
...As though demanding freedom.
As gentle as a mother's love,
I lay my lifeless find upon the soft earth
The eyes gaze at me once more then,
They close upon the Earth
And this flightless gift from a Creator
Flies, to meet her Maker.

(Have no regrets).

May 2020

I Can Hear the Earth Crying

I can hear the Earth... crying,
It cries for those who are hungry.
Fertile soil – there is food for all
Wasted in the West...
Not enough for the rest!
Obese in California, workout a 'must'!
Starving in the Yemen, intravenous drip a 'must'!

I can hear the Earth... crying
It cries for those with water, seven miles away!
Rain falls – there is enough for all.
But the West demands showers,
And green golf courses, while
The rest is parched.
Not enough for the rest!

I can hear the Earth... crying.
Its seas are choked with plastic,
Throw away the drinks bottle,
Don't think – where it will end up,
In some poor community – somewhere!
Whose women sift and sell,
A dollar a day, for survival.

I can hear the Earth crying.
Its lungs are being ripped out for temporary profit,
Homes and livelihoods – destroyed.
Habitat for the gorilla, reduced,
A certain premature death.
Gorilla today. Whose fate tomorrow?

I can hear the Earth crying.
Billions of fish in the sea.
Too many are taken out
For that gourmet meal by moonlight.
Whales for oil, cod for chips,
Monkfish is cheap, won't sell, throw it back.
The death of one fish helps destroy – Creation.

I can hear the Earth... crying.
She cries for me and you.
Our atmosphere is changing,
We can't breathe in the smog.
Sea, sky, land – threatened...
As the wealthy seek more,
It means less for the poor!

May 2020

No explanation required, I think!! Having read this piece, please write to your MP about your concerns for the planet and for the life of your grandchildren. IF WE ALL DID THIS, THERE WOULD BE A RESPONSE.

Look Mate... Don't Blame Me!!

I bought a new car the other day: it will do 130 mph.
Economical too – 25 miles to the gallon.
Oh yeh, it'll go off-road. The tyres cost 250 quid a piece.
Got a good deal on them, they were part of the lease.

We've just moved into a four-bed house, near the golf club there.
Lovely kitchen, a walk-through lounge, should take my new armchair.
Big conservatory, leads onto a patio,
Oh yes! the garden's massive, it should take our new gazebo.

Holiday – yeh, we're off to Barbados for about three weeks.
We'll go 'first class' – well I don't want to sit with all those 'geeks'.
Cruising, snorkelling and an en-suite.
Yeh... the food is great out there – as much as you can eat.
Well, I think I have earned it, don't you?
I've worked hard all my life. I've got a big caravan, too!
OK, we had a bit of luck over that insurance deal. Say no more!
But I don't think we broke the law!

Well, it's just your luck – I am no snob!
I wasn't born with no silver spoon in me gob!
My dad was bus driver, me mum a cleaner...
Left school at sixteen, yeh, did time for a minor misdemeanour!

Look, I am sorry for them over there...
But if they are poor, and they got no food, no homes, yeh, I do care.
But they should get off their backsides... and work... it's no sin,
They can build their own houses, can't they? Out of corrugated tin.

When you've got no food to feed your kids, yeh, it must be hard.
No proper home, no real job, it certainly ain't no picture postcard!
No water tap, no electricity, no gas supply,
Hmm, if that happened here there would be a real outcry.

Yeh, I give to Charity.
Gave 50 pence the other day to some 'Aid' thingy!
And I watched *Children in Need* – I felt really sorry for the little dear.
Yeh, my conscience's clear. Do you fancy another beer? (@ £3 a pint)

May 2020

Help more families to break free from poverty through our Harvest Appeal.

A Wall of Wisdom...!!

A wall is a wall is a wall!
A Garden Wall ensures privacy, security – "My Space".
Mr Churchill, when not defending our future for freedom...
... Built decorative walls for relaxation, joy and comfort.
A walled garden offers climatic protection...
Giving crops a chance to grow and prosper with a healthy outcome.

Dry stone walls fused into the Cotswold landscape.
Four, five thousand years in the making,
As natural as the limestone, hewn from the quarry.
English, safe and unassuming.
Defence against Nature itself, a pounding sea, relentless.
Eats away at millions of years of shingle land...
... But the sea wall will stop it – forever! Maybe!!

In the forgotten past, Picts put fear into the heart of Britons,
AD 122 Emperor Hadrian ordered a wall be built to keep them OUT...
unsuccessfully!
Emperor Qin Shi Huang built a wall 13,170 gruelling miles.
Though it never kept the Barbarians out.
Now the tourists flock to walk it. Just to say " I did!"

The Germans were a divided nation by a wall.
Built by the east to stop the West speaking to the East.
An Iron Curtain across Europe!
Hundreds murdered, as they made a bid for freedom.
Their memorials stand today, to the shame of politicians.

1989 saw the wall breached by 'the people '
Euphoria, as mothers kissed sons, fathers held grandchildren.

For Christianity, Islam and Judaism there is a Holy place...
... Israelis and Palestinians claim it – as their own.
A separation wall pushed through homes, livelihoods and souls.
440 miles of concrete, wire and watchtowers.
Homes and olive trees uprooted for a wall of total agony.
We continue, in this humanitarian age, to build walls of chronic division.

On America's southern border, a metal wall is going up – Now!
To keep drug dealers and itinerants OUT.
But decent people are in grave distress...
... Only seeking a better life in " The Land of the Free!!"

May 2020

Here in the UK we take walls for granted. They are everywhere, unobtrusive, unseen... In other places, this is not the case – for they control the lives of millions of people... for the whole of their lives. They divide families, work places, homes and communities. Walls NEVER work. They only destroy lives.

I Have Been Forgotten

I have been forgotten.
I am unclean.
My hands have withered.
My arms are being destroyed.
My legs no longer hold me up.
The doctor is busy now.
No one wants to know me now.
I am an embarrassment.
"Go and live over there."
The sun beats down,
My body is broken.
Water quenches my thirst.
My life will soon be over.
I have Leprosy.
I have been forgotten.

Pigeon on the Fence...

I say, yes you... Pigeon on the fence
I am going to start charging by the minute – 50 pence?
What is your defence?

WHAT??

That is my fence your posterior is on.
What legal right have you to park it there?

MY WHAT?

Your bum, my dear friend, who told you to sit there?

NOBODY... I JUST...

Well let me tell you, one more time,
That the fence you're on is not yours, it is MINE.
It states quite clearly in the deeds
That there fence which surrounds my garden
Is legally mine, if you beg my pardon.

OH... WELL...

And another thing which doesn't make sense
Is what you have been *doing* upon my fence,
For that contravenes another law.

A... WHAT?

It is called the Indecency Act of 1960.
It means you can't have sex on my fence.

LOOK MATE, HOLD ON A MO'...

No excuse, my feathered friend.
If you have sex and break that fence you'll have to pay in the end!!

LOOK, ALL I WANT TO DO IS EAT,
AND THIS FENCE, IT JUST MAKES A GREAT SEAT!

Dear Sir, if that is your defence
You still can't do it on *my* fence.
Why not go into a tree
Like a robin or a thrush...? Don't you agree?

I AM JUST A HUMBLE PIGEON, MATE,
I TRIED MY LUCK ON THAT SWING GATE.

...And I don't suppose you had much luck.

NO SIR, I DIDN'T EVEN GET A F...!!

Well, that is not my concern.
Some day my friend, you will have to learn
...That, for us to live in harmony
You can only have sex at Hogmanay!!

May 2020

Bear Necessities...
(in Teddy Bear Blue)

My Dear Vicar of St Stephen's
You must be busy for several reasons.
Lockdown has brought you problems to solve
Those at home, how do you manage to involve?
'Virtually', I expect, but if by chance it's not too late,
Get them to put 20 pound notes upon the plate?
So, as I say, I know you're very busy, Vicar dear,
But may I whisper in your ear?
You see, I am a Bear who has lost his twin!
It happened at birth, due to the fact our mother drank gin!
Whilst Daddy was serving time for smuggling,
Me and my twin we're really struggling.
Then, four years ago, almost to the day,
This bloke came in, wearing Red Shoes – and took my twin away,
Left me sitting there 'in-between',
Though eventually I was sold to the Dean.
OK, I can't complain, I sat for years in his kitchen.
Trouble was, it was like being in prison.
I dreamt every night of my bear twin,
I thought I would never see him again.
Then, one evening, when the Dean was drinking Champagne
With a very tall, elderly vicar – called Bob Payne –
I overheard them speak of YOU...
The Dean said: "I am sure, one day, she'll be Bishop of Looe.
She has a bear she took to Westcott."
Yes, it's true – I became the college mascot
But still I longed to see my twin brother,
I know he's around the Willenhall area – somewhere or other!
So, dear Vicar, of St Steve's,
If you see my twin, tell him I love him, and that I still grieve.
And, perhaps one day, we'll all meet up
And drink tea... from a China cup!

Hands of the Earth – Let's Get a Grip!!

Let's get a grip!
Famine, war, fires, pandemic, pollution, hunger, poverty,
Exclusion, extinction,
Let's get a grip!
Let us all come together under one creative God.
7.8 billion of us *could* be united. Let's get a grip!
Each one of us has been given a life
Each one of us has been given a talent...
A talent to farm, a talent to design, a talent to build.
A talent to serve, a talent to give, a talent to share.
Let's get a grip!
7.8 billion pairs of hands to...
Support, guide, nurture and pray.
So, come on – let's get a grip.
No more greed, hate, poison, bullying or bombs.
Let us – lay down our guns, our tanks, the aircraft carriers,
Gases, rifles, landmines and nuclear weapons.
Let's get a grip!
The hands of the Earth are *OUR* hands. Ready *NOW* – to:
Greet, embrace, shake, welcome.
We are ready to "Love one another" for our own future.
To smile, compromise, negotiate, 'Give' to each other.
White, black, lesbian, gay, trans, disabled, old and young.
We all come under the one banner...
The banner of – human beings.
"So, all you – dictators, tyrants, bigots, murderers,
You rapists, drug barons, abusers, burglars and fraudsters,
Sit up – *NOW ARE YOU LISTENING?*"
So, let's get a grip.
Our hands are ready to embrace global peace.
Where each one of us can live within our means,
Care for our children, in the lands of our birth.
Where 70 million refugees can return home to build a life for themselves and
generations to come.
Where none of us go hungry where all are educated.
Where clean... fresh water is ours – by right.
Where we respect one another for who we are.
Come on, let's smile, laugh and enjoy one another's company.
Let's live peaceably on land which was given to *ALL*,

For *WE* are in charge now – not you... but, believe it or not,
We will forgive you and also, love you, forever.
Let's get a grip!!

September 2020

Old Mick

Life is being spelt out in his craggy, windswept expression...
Furrows as deep as a newly ploughed field span his forehead...
Eyebrows, thick, grey – as a squirrel's tail.
Sunken, deep into the skull, grained eyes, the colour of midnight,
Are concealed by mottled eyelids, forever flickering...
His pitted cheeks are sullen – the right, disfigured by an ancient scar of youth.
Romans, down the centuries, have marked out a nose...
...This one has been weathered by a life outdoors...
...Alcohol has played its role in colouration – red as Rudolph's!!
Above his thin, cracked lips sits a once-handsome moustache...
...But now, grey, unkempt like a battleship in the scrapyard,
And to cap this landscape, concealing a mop of thin grey hair,
Is a 1969 Christmas gift of Harris tweed headgear.

The once tall, upright stance, has now given way to hunched shoulders...
...A defined stoop resembles an ash, in a westerly wind.
His shirt does not appeared to have seen Persil since the last Doomsday.
A 1950s grey tank-top is covered by a cheap tweed jacket,
The pockets act as his workshop – screws, nails, scissors and pliers,
...And piece of green string...
...Are always at hand: "Never know when you need 'um!!"
His worn corduroy trousers were past their sell-by date twenty years ago.

They are secured in place, by more green string – unseen, but doing its duty!!
As do the threadbare socks, concealed inside black, heavy second-hand
ex-army boots...
... They served in The Falklands, Northern Ireland and Iraq!!
Now they are starved of polish, and cow-pat has replaced the shine!!
'Old Mick' spends his day wandering the hills of the Staffordshire moorlands
With a stout stick of elder... he crosses grassland and bog.
He surveys the empty landscape for his sheep... 12 these days.
Any distressed lambs are put into his cheap tweed jacket:
The beat of his heart sustains them, until they reach the fireside of the pub.
Josie then takes over and brings the helpless mites back from the brink...
Old Mick's second love is his 'New Hampshire' chickens...
They roam free in the lower field, where fox studies them from willow bank!!
Mick scatters the feed far and wide, eggs collected each evening at five!!
Sold to locals... or given away... "Don't make no difference to me!!"
Old Gran' then has to be dealt with too!!
She grazes in the top field. Fetched in at four – milked by five, in 'barn at six.
So, as twilight falls and starlings go into murmuration,
– The pub opens 6.30... Old Mick, their first customer.
A pewter tankard has been behind the bar for 60 years, is on the bar, waiting!
Conversation is not Mick's game. Listening to 'tickle-tackle' is his art.
At 7.30, as the place gradually fills with youngsters, 'Old Mick' slips away...
... From the noise of laughter, topical talk, sexy innuendos...
Just 300 yards, to the cottage where he was born 83 years ago next Friday.
A cold beef pie, and a cold boiled egg, for his tea!!...
The day is done, for 'Old Mick'.
"Good Night, my old mate... sleep well..."

November 2020

Michael Ingle Charles Kenwood, DOB: 28/3/1937
Some people are taken for granted. They are like a moving landmark. When they are
there, we take no notice. When they are gone, we miss them!!